Greek Mythology

An Enthralling Overview of Greek Myths Gods and Goddesses

(A captivating guide to Greek Myths of Greek Gods Heroes and Monsters)

Brett Rivera

Published By **Elena Holly**

Brett Rivera

All Rights Reserved

Greek Mythology: An Enthralling Overview of Greek Myths Gods and Goddesses (A captivating guide to Greek Myths of Greek Gods Heroes and Monsters)

ISBN   978-1-9992319-8-9

Legal & Disclaimer

The information contained in this book is not designed to replace or take the place of any form of medicine or professional medical advice. The information in this book has been provided for educational & entertainment purposes only.

The information contained in this book has been compiled from sources deemed reliable, and it is accurate to the best of the Author's knowledge; however, the Author cannot guarantee its accuracy and validity and cannot be held liable for any errors or omissions. Changes are periodically made to this book. You must consult your doctor or get professional medical advice before using any of the suggested remedies, techniques, or information in this book.

Table Of Contents

Chapter 1: The Genesis Of The Greek Universe

In the primordial expanse of Chaos, wherein the very essence of life danced in formless waves, the Greek creation fable takes root— an implementing overture that resonates thru the corridors of time. From this infinite void emerged Gaia, the Earth, and Eros, the airy embodiment of affection and choice. A cosmic ballet unfold out as Gaia and Uranus, the celestial sky, gave starting to a pantheon of formidable beings—Titans, Cyclopes, and Hecatonchires, entities decorated with one hundred palms and fifty heads.

Nevertheless, the looming fear of the powerful strength inside their offspring grabbed Uranus. In his worry, he imprisoned the Cyclopes and Hecatonchires in the cavernous depths of the Earth. Gaia, the nurturing mom, felt the pain of her captive kids and devised a formidable plan to free up them. Turning to her youngest son, Cronus, endowed with foxy and ambition, Gaia sought a champion for her cause.

Guided with the resource of the understanding of Gaia, Cronus released into a daring quest, decreasing Uranus and assuming the mantle of Titan rulership. From the spilled blood of Uranus, alchemy of creation took place, birthing the Furies, the Giants, and the Meliae—nymphs of the ash trees—manifestations of nature's raw power.

Cronus, uniting collectively collectively along with his sister Rhea, ascended to rule the Titans. Yet, shadows of prophecy haunted Cronus, whispering of a future wherein his personal offspring might emulate his rebellion towards Uranus. Driven via using this ominous foresight, Cronus succumbed to a darkish compulsion—devouring his very very own children, Hestia, Demeter, Hera, Hades, and Poseidon, as they drew their first breaths.

However, even as Rhea bore their sixth infant, Zeus, a spark of rise up ignited internal her. In a clandestine act of defiance, Rhea secretively birthed Zeus and provided Cronus with a stone swathed in swaddling clothes. Deceived, Cronus consumed the stone whole, unknowingly sparing Zeus from the lousy future that happened his siblings.

Zeus, hid inside the cocoon of secrecy, matured right into a god of prodigious might also. As the cosmic degree awaited, Zeus confronted his father, compelling him to regurgitate his swallowed participants of the family. The battleground of the gods, the Titanomachy, opened up—a decade-prolonged struggle wherein Zeus and his divine brethren, aided thru the Cyclopes and Hecatonchires, clashed in the direction of the Titans.

The heavens resounded with thunder, and the earth quivered below the celestial warfare. In the end, the more youthful gods emerged a hit, banishing the defeated Titans to Tartarus—the abyssal depths of the Underworld.

With the Titans vanquished, Zeus, along his siblings, the Cyclopes, and the Hecatonchires, ascended to the regal heights of Mount Olympus. Zeus, the ideally fitted deity, seized dominion over the heavens, Poseidon ruled the big seas, and Hades reigned over the shadowed Underworld.

Thus, the Greek introduction myth unraveled the cosmic symphony—the genesis of the universe, the ascent of the Olympian gods, and the carving of their divine geographical areas. It unveiled the prologue to the captivating stories woven for the duration of Greek mythology—a labyrinthine tapestry where gods, heroes, and mortals navigate the elaborate interplay of divine strength, human aspirations, and the complexities of the historical Greek international.

The Titans and the Olympians

The Titans are essential figures in Greek mythology, serving as excellent deities earlier than the mythical rule of the Olympians. Born from the celestial union of Gaia, the Earth, and Uranus, the sky, the Titans emerged as ambitious beings in the course of the fabled Golden Age, their should in all likelihood interwoven with the very cloth of the natural global.

At the helm of this divine cohort become Cronus, the youngest scion of Gaia and Uranus, main twelve of the maximum eminent Titans into an era of extraordinary electricity and cosmic effect. These huge figures included Oceanus, the personification of the boundless ocean; Tethys, the serene embodiment of freshwater and consort to Oceanus; Hyperion, the radiant pressure related to the sun; Theia, a celestial presence related to the moon; Coeus, the highbrow architect; Phoebe, a prophetic determine shaping future; Rhea, sister and spouse to Cronus; Themis, the figure of divine law and order; Mnemosyne, the ethereal embodiment of memory; Crius, the overseer of constellations; Iapetus, intertwined with mortal lifestyles; and Cronus' sister-spouse, a strong Titaness variously named Philyra or Rhea, destined to starting the Olympians.

Yet, a palpable fear seized Cronus—a trepidation rooted in an ominous prophecy forecasting his overthrow by using his progeny. To thwart destiny, Cronus enacted a sinister ceremony, devouring each of his new child kids, save Zeus, hidden away in secrecy and raised past the Titan's ominous attain.

The cosmic degree for this reason set, Zeus, the destiny sovereign of the Olympians, confronted Cronus, compelling the Titan to regurgitate his divine siblings. The ensuing struggle, called the Titanomachy, unfolded with celestial grandeur. Assisted by using using the bold Cyclopes and the brilliant Hecatonchires, the nascent Olympians emerged positive, consigning the defeated Titans to the unfathomable abyss of Tartarus.

he Olympians, having strong down the Titans, ascended to their celestial thrones, heralding a present day technology of divine governance. Zeus, the thunderous deity, assumed the mantle of high-quality ruler. Alongside him, his siblings and allies claimed dominion over the cosmos—Poseidon, the tempestuous god of the seas; Hades, the shadowed lord of the Underworld; Hera, the queen of the gods; Demeter, the bountiful goddess of agriculture; and Hestia, the serene determine of the fireplace.

This pantheon of twelve Olympians, respected and worshipped via using the ancient Greeks, presided over the hard tapestry of human lifestyles and the natural worldwide. Within this divine ensemble, personalities spread out with putting variety—from the sagacious Athena to the passionate Ares—providing profound glimpses into the intricacies of the human psyche.

The battle among Titans and Olympians, and the subsequent Olympian ascendancy, etched a large addition in the annals of Greek mythology. It symbolized greater than a trifling transfer of celestial authority—it embodied the eternal rhythm of electricity dynamics, the ceaseless war amongst order and chaos, rebel and dominion, echoing thru the undying corridors of divine authority in the captivating worldwide of Greek fantasy.

The Role of Chaos in Greek Mythology

Chaos is the silent architect of creation in Greek mythology, a amazing emptiness that precedes the advent of gods and the very material of the cosmos. More than a mere concept, Chaos is each the foundation and the embodiment of limitless ability, a formless chasm from which all things emerged.

Imagine a large and shapeless void, a cosmic canvas without shape or discernible elements – this is Chaos. It is a dark abyss, an empty expanse that precedes the notions of Earth, heavens, and time itself. Within Chaos, there aren't any barriers, no order; it's far the final expression of formlessness and ambiguity, a cosmic womb pregnant with the possibilities of introduction.

From this primordial Chaos, the primary stirrings of the cosmos manifested. Gaia, the Earth; Tartarus, the abyss below; and Eros, the primal strain of affection and desire, emerged, setting the extent for the grand drama of introduction. Gaïa, mainly, accomplished a pivotal characteristic, giving begin to Titans, gods, and the physical global, weaving the tough net of lifestyles.

Chaos, however, isn't merely the inspiration of factors; it's far the starting area itself. Erebus and Nyx, offspring of Chaos, similarly expanded the divine lineage, representing darkness and night time, respectively, and giving shipping to a huge variety of deities. In the great tapestry of Greek cosmogony, Chaos isn't always a aware being; it is the fundamental stress, the essence from which gods and the cosmos sprang forth.

This concept of Chaos serves multifaceted roles in Greek mythology. Firstly, it narrates the mysterious origins of the universe, offering a framework for the inception of the arena. Secondly, it underscores the touchy stability amongst order and sickness, emphasizing the perpetual war of gods and heroes to deliver harmony to the cosmos.

Yet, Chaos is extra than a story device; it symbolizes the cosmos's vastness and intricacy, representing the inherent unpredictability of existence. It emphasizes the boundaries of mortal statistics, reminding us of the awe-inspiring mysteries that lie past our comprehension.

Chapter 2: The Twelve Olympians Gods

The Twelve Olympians are the distinguished deities in Greek mythology, every controlling a separate territory that molds the mortal and heavenly spheres; those official gods and goddesses, perched upon their thrones atop Mount Olympus, weave a tale of power, intrigue, and function an impact on that resonates via the annals of Greek fable.

1. Zeus - King of the Gods

Zeus, the paramount discern in the pantheon, assumes the mantle of the very nice ruler and leader of the Olympians. A regal deity, Zeus wields thunderbolts and governs from his celestial throne, presiding over the heavens with unrivaled authority.

a. God of the Sky and Thunder: Zeus instructions the very factors, reigning over the sky and Its phenomena. His presence is felt inside the roaring thunder and the flashing lightning, an imposing display of divine power.

b. Upholder of Justice: As the arbiter of justice, Zeus ensures the enforcement of divine regulation and order. He metes out punishment to wrongdoers, rewards the virtuous, and oversees oaths and contracts with an unwavering enjoy of equity.

c. Protector of Guests and Supplicants: The customer of hospitality, Zeus guards the sacred covenant among host and traveller. In his benevolence, he guarantees the protection of vacationers and extends safety to those trying to find secure haven or sanctuary.

d. Divine Intervention: Zeus, the orchestrator of fate, intervenes in mortal affairs. His choices endure the weight of benefits or punishments, shaping the destinies of humans and towns alike.

e. Father of Gods and Mortals: With a prolific lineage, Zeus fathers a pantheon of divine and heroic offspring. Apollo, Artemis, Hermes, Athena, Perseus, and Hercules are a few of the illustrious progeny of his severa liaisons with goddesses and mortal ladies.

f. Symbol of Power and Authority: A picture of majestic authority, Zeus is frequently portrayed on a throne, wielding a scepter and thunderbolt. The eagle, o.K.Tree, and thunderbolt stand as enduring symbols of his dominion.

Zeus's have an effect on is going past being a deity with character attributes and emerges as a crucial figure in limitless myths and legends. Engaging in epic conflicts, workout best authority, and interacting with every gods and mortals, Zeus epitomizes the tricky and frequently fierce courting between divine beings and humanity. The narratives of his exploits underscore the grandeur and strength inherent inside the divine realm, weaving a tapestry that unfolds with each thunderous decree from the king of the gods.

2. Hera - Queen of the Gods

In the divine tapestry of Greek mythology, Hera stands as an excellent determine, the queen of the gods, and the esteemed consort of Zeus. Radiating majesty and strength, she is a multifaceted deity, intricately woven into the material of the Olympian pantheon.

a. Goddess of Marriage: Hera, with her divine authority, presides over the sacred business corporation of marriage and childbirth. She is the symbolic dad or mum of wedded unions, bestowing advantages upon marriages and ensuring the fidelity and harmony of spousal relationships.

b. Queen of the Gods: In her union with Zeus, Hera ascends to the lofty role of queen of the gods. Her regal have an effect on extends in some unspecified time inside the destiny of the divine realm, and she actively participates inside the choice-making techniques that form the route of Olympian affairs.

c. Protector of Women and Children: Embracing a maternal position, Hera turns into a vigilant dad or mum of ladies and children, specially the ones born in the sanctity of marriage. Mothers invoke her protecting presence during childbirth, seeking out her assist and safeguarding.

d. Punisher of Infidelity: Hera, bearing witness to Zeus's severa infidelities, manifests as a goddess of every jealousy and vengeance. Fiercely protecting of her honor, she metes out retribution toward Zeus's fanatics and their progeny, weaving trials and tribulations into their lives.

e. Patron of Women's Roles: Hera encapsulates the traditional beliefs of femininity and girls's roles in historical Greek society. Her essence symbolizes a accomplice's loyalty, devotion to circle of relatives, and the upkeep of the family—a illustration of societal expectancies positioned upon girls.

f. Divine Intervention: Engaging actively in mortal affairs, Hera intervenes in topics concerning marriage, fidelity, and family. Her interventions supply each rewards and punishments, with mortals becoming recipients of her want or subjects of her divine wrath based totally on their actions and adherence to her mind.

g. Symbols and Representations: Hera's regal presence is often depicted adorned with a crown or diadem, wielding a scepter that suggests her authority. The peacock, cow, and pomegranate emerge as her symbolic companions, embodying splendor, fertility, and nurturing components.

Despite the complexities springing up from her relationship with Zeus and espresso acts of retribution, Hera remains an influential and revered deity in the Greek pantheon. She personifies the beliefs and challenges inherent within the organisation of marriage, the nuanced roles of girls in historic society, and the preservation of family and family—a testament to the difficult interplay of divine dynamics and their impact on mortal lives.

3. Poseidon - Master of the Deep

Poseidon seems as a effective man or woman within the extensive material of Greek mythology, ruling first-rate over the huge expanses of the sea. His affect, much like the undulating waves he commands, extends beyond the maritime realm, shaping both the natural worldwide and the destinies of mortals. Here, we delve into the multifaceted aspects and giant obligations that define Poseidon, the god of the ocean.

a. God of the Sea: Poseidon's sovereign place is the ocean, an empire that encompasses oceans, seas, rivers, and lakes. His dominion extends to the very depths of aquatic geographical areas, in which he holds sway over-currents, tides, and the ebb and float of the ocean's might probably.

b. Earthshaker: Reverberating with seismic electricity, Poseidon is aptly hailed due to the fact the "Earthshaker." His formidable abilties encompass the functionality to unleash earthquakes, shake the pointers of the land,

and emphasize his dominion over each sea and earth.

c. Patron of Seafarers: As the god of the ocean, Poseidon assumes the critical role of patron and protector of sailors, seafarers, and fishermen. Those embarking on perilous maritime trips invoke his name, offering prayers and sacrifices for strong voyages and tranquil seas, looking for his benevolent choose.

d. God of Horses: Poseidon's affinity with horses is first rate, incomes him the esteemed call of the god of horses and horsemanship. He is credited with the advent of the first horse and is often depicted astride a chariot, drawn through excellent sea creatures or horses.

e. Creator of Springs and Fountains: The divine touch of Poseidon extends to the terrestrial realm, wherein he holds the power to create springs, fountains, and wells. His effect over freshwater sources underscores the significance of these existence-giving factors.

f. Shaper of Landscapes: Beyond the sea's aspect, Poseidon wields the energy to shape and mold the land itself. He can craft coastlines, forge islands, and orchestrate modifications in the natural topography, showcasing his omnipotence over every land and sea.

g. Symbol of Power and Authority: A trident, with its three-pronged tines, serves as the long-lasting photograph of Poseidon's dominion. This formidable weapon now not only represents his command over the ocean but additionally stands as a powerful photograph of his unequalled power and authority a few of the Olympian gods.

Poseidon's have an impact on transcends the limits of his ocean realm, weaving into the complex narratives of Greek mythology. His man or woman embodies the capricious and bold forces of the natural international, echoing the significance of the ocean inside the lives of ancient Greeks who relied on maritime sports activities for exchange, exploration, and sustenance.

Within the pantheon of Olympian deities, Poseidon stays a reputable and imposing figure, commemorated with the useful resource of folks that navigate the unpredictable seas and rely upon its sources for their livelihoods. His memories upload profound depth to the wealthy tapestry of Greek mythology, revealing the interconnectedness of gods, mortals, and the ever-unpredictable forces of nature.

four. Demeter - Guardian of the Harvest and Life's Bounty

Greek mythology offers Demeter as a especially esteemed deity who personifies the essence of fertility, agriculture, and the cyclical issue of existence. Her multifaceted characteristic encompasses now not incredible the cultivation of plants but additionally the nurturing of existence in its diverse office work. Let's discover the severa aspects and responsibilities that define Demeter, the benevolent goddess who bestows abundance upon the earth.

a. Goddess of Agriculture: At the middle of Demeter's have an impact on lies her characteristic because the goddess of agriculture and the harvest. Her watchful gaze ensures the fertility of the earth, making high quality the success of crop increase, the richness of the harvest, and the prosperity of agricultural pastimes.

b. Bringer of Seasons: Demeter's tale intricately intertwines with the converting seasons, reflecting the profound connection among her emotional nation and the earth's fertility. The cycles of grief and satisfaction, reflected in the abduction and go back of her daughter Persephone from the Underworld, convey in the advent of seasons, marking the ebb and go with the flow of existence.

c. Protector of Grain and Crops: Farmers and cultivators invoke Demeter for her benevolence in overseeing the cultivation of grains and flowers. Wheat, barley, and corn fall beneath her shielding gaze, and her divine have an effect on guarantees the abundance and fulfillment of agricultural endeavors.

d. Nurturer of Life: Beyond her function in agriculture, Demeter extends her care to all residing matters. Her nurturing contact fosters the nicely-being of every flora and animals, emphasizing the interconnectedness of existence and the significance of preserving the sensitive balance of the natural global.

e. Goddess of Sacred Law: Demeter assumes the feature of a guardian of sacred law and order, upholding ideas of fairness, justice, and the right observance of rituals and traditions. Her presence is invoked during ceremonies and agricultural fairs, reinforcing the sacred bond between humans and the divine.

f. Mysteries of Eleusis: Demeter's have an impact on extends to the sacred rituals of Eleusis, wherein the mysterious Eleusinian Mysteries had been celebrated. These secretive rites promised religious salvation and a cushty afterlife, further cementing Demeter's characteristic within the profound components of Greek spiritual practices.

g. Symbol of Motherly Love: The poignant relationship among Demeter and her daughter, Persephone, serves as a poignant picture of motherly love. The narrative of Demeter's relentless search for Persephone after her abduction via Hades epitomizes the depths of a mom's love and the iconic choice for reunion.

Demeter's importance in ancient Greek society is going past the agricultural region. She represents the interconnectedness amongst humanity and the herbal global, together together with her worship and reverence reflecting gratitude for the earth's fertility and the sustenance it graciously presents. In Demeter, the Greeks decided not best a mum or dad of the harvest but furthermore a nurturing pressure that perpetuated the cycles of existence and growth.

5. Athena - Wisdom, Warfare, and Civilizational Prowess

In the illustrious tapestry of Greek mythology, Athena stands as a beacon of know-how, strategic acumen, and innovative finesse. This reputable goddess, embodying a large number of attributes and duties, performs a pivotal role in shaping the beliefs and values of historic Greek society. Let's delve into the severa elements that define Athena's influential presence inside the pantheon.

a. Goddess of Wisdom: Athena's primary affiliation is with cognizance, records, and highbrow pursuits. She symbolizes strategic intelligence, rational thinking, and prudent choice-making. Often portrayed as a practical counselor, Athena extends her mentorship to every heroes and mortals, guiding them with sagacity.

b. Patron of Warfare and Strategic Warfare: While Athena is a goddess of warfare, her location transcends mere fight; she embodies strategic war, emphasizing disciplined strategies over sheer pressure. Athena champions strategic making plans, military intelligence, and courage on the battlefield, making her the sought-after customer for the ones valuing knowledge in warfare.

c. Protector of Cities and Civilizations: Athena assumes the important role of mother or father and protector of towns and civilizations. Revered due to the fact the "polis" goddess, she suggests the significance of order, governance, and the guideline of thumb of law in human society. Athena imparts her information to metropolis-states, fostering simply governance and societal harmony.

d. Goddess of Crafts and the Arts: Beyond the realms of conflict and know-how, Athena is an inspiring strain in craftsmanship and the humanities. She serves due to the reality the consumer of severa crafts, consisting of weaving, pottery, sculpture, and architecture. Artisans and craftsmen are looking for her pick for creativity and expertise in their endeavors.

e. Guardian of Heroes: Athena assumes the characteristic of protector and consumer of heroes. Her divine steerage and help empower heroes at the side of Perseus, Odysseus, and Hercules, providing them with strategic advocate, bravery, and assist on their quests.

f. Symbol of Female Empowerment: Athena stands as a powerful and impartial goddess, tough conventional gender roles. Her character exemplifies lady energy, know-how, and strategic wondering, breaking free from societal stereotypes. Athena turns into a beacon of empowerment and intellectual hobbies for women.

g. Symbols and Representations: Athena is frequently depicted wearing a helmet and carrying a guard, spear, or sword—symbols of her affiliation with warfare and strategic thinking. The owl, symbolizing know-how and understanding, stands as her sacred animal, representing her vigilant and insightful nature.

Athena's have an impact on extends an extended way beyond the area of the gods, shaping the moral compass and aspirations of historic Greek society. Her harmonious integration of information, courage, and creativity emphasizes the importance of intellectual hobbies, strategic wondering, and the pursuit of justice. Athena's worship serves as a testomony to the profound effect of her beliefs at the cultural material of historic Greece.

6. Apollo - Radiant Patron of Arts and Harmony

In the illustrious tapestry of Greek mythology, Apollo, the god of the sun, moderate, prophecy, track, and recovery, stands as a radiant and multifaceted deity. His numerous array of attributes and obligations encapsulates numerous sides of human lifestyles, shaping him right right right into a respected determine within the Olympian pantheon. Let us delve into the intricacies of Apollo's person, every aspect contributing to his prominence within the geographical regions of each gods and mortals.

a. God of the Sun: Apollo's association with the solar elevates him to the recognition of a lifestyles-bringer and illuminator. Guiding his celestial chariot at some point of the sky, Apollo symbolizes enlightenment, readability, and the relentless pursuit of information. The solar, underneath Apollo's area, turns into a metaphor for the pursuit of reality and information.

b. Patron of the Arts: The resonating chords of Apollo's lyre echo through the innovative realms, organising him due to the fact the purchaser of the arts. From song to poetry and the great arts, Apollo inspires creativity and serves as a muse to artists. His have an impact on extends to the Muses, and goddesses of creative expression, making him the embodiment of revolutionary belief.

c. God of Prophecy: Apollo's enigmatic oracles, most significantly at Delphi, feature him because of the truth the god of prophecy. Seekers flocked to the Pythia, Apollo's priestess, to glean insights into the future. Apollo's present of prophecy converted him right right into a respected manual, offering facts and foresight to the ones navigating the unpredictable currents of destiny.

d. Healer and God of Medicine: Apollo's healing touch and association with medicinal drug growth him to a divine clinical physician. The Rod of Asclepius, a personnel entwined with a serpent, symbolizes his recovery powers. Temples devoted to Apollo served as sanctuaries for the sick, emphasizing his role as a benevolent healer.

e. Protector of Flocks and Herds: In the pastoral geographical areas, Apollo emerges as a father or mother, overseeing the nicely-being of flocks and herds. His effect extends to the fertility and abundance of cattle, forging a connection maximum of the divine and the natural global.

f. God of Athletics and Sports: Apollo's agile prowess extends to the region of athleticism, patronizing sports activities sports competitions. Archery, song, and chariot racing discover choice in his area, as he embodies the pursuit of bodily excellence and the grace that accompanies such endeavors.

g. Symbol of Harmony and Balance: Apollo's enduring legacy consists of embodying the beliefs of order, stability, and moderation. The idea of the "golden endorse" reveals resonance in his teachings, urging a harmonious life with the aid of navigating the sensitive equilibrium among extremes.

Apollo's multifaceted nature weaves a tapestry that shows the severa elements of human enjoy. From the brilliance of the sun to the harmonies of ingenious expression, Apollo's have an impact on lengthy-hooked up historical Greek society, emphasizing the significance of stability, progressive pursuits, and the perpetual quest for enlightenment. As the radiant client of arts and harbinger of focus, Apollo remains a photo of concept for those meaning to mild up the arena with creativity and information.

7. Artemis - Enchanting Huntress of the Wild and Moonlit Skies

Artemis, the goddess of the quest, wildness, and the moon, emerges as an tremendous and liked person inside the extensive fabric of Greek mythology. Her essence, brimming with independence, athleticism, and a profound connection to nature, weaves a story that transcends the divine realm. Let's resolve the myriad factors and duties that define Artemis, painting a portrait of this mesmerizing deity.

a. Goddess of the Hunt: Artemis reigns exceptional within the realm of searching, displaying exceptional information with bow and arrow. A vital hunter, she safeguards the delicate balance of the wild, reputable no longer wonderful for her prowess but moreover as a protector of natural worldwide and the sanctity of untamed landscapes.

b. Protector of the Wilderness: As a parent of the desolate tract, Artemis watches over the untouched expanses of the earth, from dense forests to rugged mountains. Her affect ensures the upkeep of nature, fostering the harmonious coexistence of plant life and fauna in their herbal habitats.

c. Goddess of the Moon: The moon, with its mystical appeal and transformative stages, unearths an embodiment in Artemis. Whether decorated with a crescent moon crown or guiding her moon chariot through the celestial expanse, Artemis symbolizes the cyclical nature of existence and channels the lady energies of the lunar realm.

Chapter 3: The Heroes And Their Stories

Heracles (Hercules) and his Twelve Labors

In the illustrious Greek fable, Heracles, better identified with the aid of his Roman counterpart Hercules, emerges as a huge determine—a paragon of strength, resilience, and indomitable will. His journey is intricately woven with divine interventions, widespread adversaries, and the onerous penance of the Twelve Labors.

1. Slaughter of the Nemean Lion

Heracles, the renowned hero of Greek mythology, launched into a huge quest as a part of his twelve labors, a penance for past transgressions. His inaugural ordeal, the slaying of the Nemean Lion, unfold out as a testomony to his exquisite electricity and tactical brilliance. The Nemean Lion, a worry within the area of Nemea, supplied an splendid venture with its invulnerable nature, decorated in golden fur that confounded mortal guns.

Undeterred by means of using the lion's legendary invincibility, Heracles, armed with awesome power and foxy, tracked the beast to its treacherous cave. The brutal disagreement that ensued examined the hero's unwavering self-control to triumph over reputedly insurmountable odds.

Heracles, to start with looking to pierce the lion's impervious cowl with arrows, determined conventional weaponry futile in opposition to the creature's golden defenses. Faced with this impasse, the hero, recognised for each his bodily might also and thoughts, devised a very particular method.

The battle escalated right into a raw display of strength as Heracles engaged the lion in a brutal and constant struggle. Understanding that traditional weaponry became insufficient, he shifted techniques. The hero, drawing upon his divine lineage, grappled with the beast, leveraging his brilliant strength to gain dominance. In a moment of sheer also can, he determined on an unconventional method – the use of his bare arms, Heracles strangled the Nemean Lion, overcoming its legendary invulnerability.

Having triumphed over the formidable foe, Heracles did now not genuinely declare victory; he verified resourcefulness in utilizing the lion's very very very own ambitious claws. The hero meticulously skinned the creature and customary a shielding cloak from its impenetrable hide. This symbolic trophy not great showcased his victory however additionally served as a tangible reminder of his prowess.

The slaying of the Nemean Lion marked the initiation of Heracles' twelve labors, a sequence of fantastic trials that might check his mettle and resilience. This first hard work set the tone for subsequent feats, putting in place Heracles as a paragon of heroism, fearlessness, and flexibility. The legend echoed via the a long time, immortalizing Heracles as a hero able to overcoming apparently unbeatable worrying conditions thru a harmonious aggregate of energy and wit.

2. Slaying of the Lernaean Hydra

Heracles, the indomitable hero of Greek delusion, encountered every specific formidable project in his mythical quest – the slaying of the Lernaean Hydra, a sizable serpent-like creature with the precise ability to regenerate heads. This creature, living within the ominous swamps of Lerna, posed a dangerous hazard to the encircling regions, with its venom able to causing short and lethal harm.

Heracles approached this labor with a recognition of the hydra's extraordinary capability to multiply its heads. The project became in addition complex via the creature's relentless regeneration – for every head severed, greater sprouted in its vicinity. Undeterred by the reputedly insurmountable odds, Heracles enlisted the useful resource of his nephew, Iolaus, to confront this legendary risk.

To outwit the Hydra, Heracles formulated a strategic method. Armed with a sword or membership, he may additionally sever the creature's heads even as Iolaus played a critical feature in cauterizing the exposed neck stumps with fireside. This innovative method avoided the hydra from perpetuating its reputedly endless cycle of regeneration.

The already ambitious undertaking took an extra flip whilst a sizeable crab, an ally of the Hydra, joined the fray. The crab continuously attacked Heracles' feet, introducing a modern-day layer of complexity to the conflict. Demonstrating not quality strength but moreover resourcefulness, Heracles managed to conquer this extra task by way of the usage of using decisively crushing the crab below his foot, neutralizing the threat it posed.

Ultimately, Heracles emerged positive in the conflict in opposition to the Lernaean Hydra thru methodically cutting off all its heads and the use of fireplace to make certain they could not regenerate. To seal the creature's future, he buried the handiest immortal head, rendering it inaccessible. This heroic victory showcased Heracles' functionality to strategize, adapt, and triumph over reputedly insurmountable limitations.

In a symbolic gesture of his conquest, Heracles dipped his arrows into the Hydra's venom, imbuing them with a deadly efficiency. This strategic bypass introduced a robust arsenal to his weaponry, proving useful in next adventures. The slaying of the Lernaean Hydra stands as a testomony to Heracles' bravery, ability, and resourcefulness, solidifying its vicinity as one of the maximum celebrated exploits in his storied heroic profession.

three. Capture the Golden Hind of Artemis

The tough and sensitive undertaking of seizing Artemis' Golden Hind became certainly one of Heracles' twelve epic labors. The Golden Hind, furthermore referred to as the Golden Stag or Ceryneian Hind, become no normal deer; it bore golden antlers and held sacred significance as a prized possession of the goddess Artemis, the revered deity of the hunt. Tasked with shooting this speedy and sacred creature, Heracles entered a realm in which potential, persistence, and worldwide own family members have become paramount.

The capture of the Golden Hind supplied a completely specific set of demanding conditions. Artemis, due to the fact the goddess of the hunt and protector of flora and fauna, had a special affinity for this sacred deer. Heracles end up entrusted with the undertaking of taking snap shots the Hind with out inflicting them harm, a assignment requiring each physical prowess and finesse.

Undertaking a prolonged and demanding hunt, Heracles showed his staying electricity and perseverance. The Golden Hind, famend for its terrific tempo and agility, led Heracles on a 365 days-prolonged pursuit, trying out the hero's tracking abilties and determination.

Finally, after an prolonged period of tracking and pursuit, Heracles succeeded in cornering the elusive Golden Hind. With tremendous staying power and skills, he approached the sacred creature, ensuring that the capture have become completed without inflicting damage. Accounts describe Heracles lightly immobilizing the Hind, every cradling it in his palms or the use of ropes to secure it, showcasing his capability to navigate the sensitive assignment with precision.

However, the capture did not arise without outcomes. Artemis, the divine mother or father of the Golden Hind, regarded in advance than Heracles, expressing her displeasure on the seize of her sacred deer. In this important 2d, Heracles exhibited now not only bodily prowess but additionally global family members and knowledge. He defined to Artemis the need of taking pix the Golden Hind as a part of his penance, assuring her that the creature is probably launched unhurt after being furnished to King Eurystheus, his taskmaster.

Impressed thru Heracles' appreciate and clarification, Artemis acquiesced, allowing him to keep with the captured deer. With the touchy scenario navigated efficiently, Heracles lower lower back the Golden Hind to King Eurystheus, supplying it as proof of the effective very last contact of his hard work.

The seize of the Golden Hind stands as a testomony to Heracles' multifaceted skills. Beyond showcasing his hunter's talent and physical prowess, it highlights his resourcefulness, staying energy, and diplomatic acumen in managing touchy situations related to divine entities. This tough work in addition solidified Heracles' popularity as a legendary hero in Greek mythology, able to undertaking apparently now not viable obligations with a combination of electricity, intelligence, and finesse.

4. Capturing the Erymanthian Boar

In the pursuit of his twelve labors, Heracles faced the formidable assignment of capturing the Erymanthian Boar, a big and ferocious creature wreaking havoc at the slopes of Mount Erymanthus. This labor may additionally want to test no longer only Heracles' electricity and courage but additionally his ability to strategize and conquer surprising obstacles.

The adventure to Mount Erymanthus proved treacherous as Heracles encountered the centaurs, half of of-human and 1/2 of-horse beings infamous for his or her unruly nature. These creatures, led with the resource of using the centaur Pholus, attempted to prevent Heracles' development. Undeterred, Heracles employed his sizeable power and wit to conquer the resistance posed via the centaurs, allowing him to press earlier in his quest.

Upon reaching Mount Erymanthus, Heracles faced the daunting undertaking of taking photos the boar. The creature, wild and ferocious, posed a sizeable danger. Heracles, however, displayed his strategic acumen. In one model of the parable, he chased the boar into deep snow, at the identical time as in every different, he led it right into a thick layer of dust. In every situations, the boar have come to be trapped and exhausted, permitting Heracles to capitalize on its weakened usa.

With tremendous bodily prowess, Heracles subdued the Erymanthian Boar, binding its legs and securing it for the adventure decrease once more to King Eurystheus. However, the undertaking did no longer give up with the seize of the formidable creature. King Eurystheus, intimidated by the sight of the fearsome boar, sought safe haven in a large bronze jar upon Heracles' approach, adding an unexpected and comical twist to the difficult paintings.

The seize of the Erymanthian Boar showcased Heracles' multifaceted capabilities. His courage and bodily strength were obvious within the face of an outstanding opponent, but similarly critical became his strategic wondering in trapping and subduing the boar.

Additionally, the tough work highlighted Heracles' mastery over dangerous creatures, a normal topic in his mythological exploits.

This feat further solidified Heracles' popularity as a mythical hero in Greek mythology, able to confronting and overcoming traumatic conditions that mixed bodily prowess with intellect. The Erymanthian Boar, with its precise twists and turns, delivered a few other illustrious economic catastrophe to the epic tale of Heracles and his extremely good twelve labors.

five. Clean the Augean Stables

Heracles faced the large system of cleaning the Augean Stables as part of his famed twelve labors, a large venture that challenged now not best his electricity but moreover his inventiveness. These stables, owned thru King Augeas, had grow to be a cesspool of dust and manure because of the massive form of livestock housed inner.

The sheer scale of the venture appeared insurmountable. The stables had been great, and the accumulated dirt presented a frightening undertaking. However, Heracles, identified for his resourcefulness, devised a plan that showcased his capacity to count on past conventional techniques.

Rather than trying the laborious and time-eating venture of manually casting off the manure, Heracles grew to become to the forces of nature. He harnessed the energy of water to cleanse the Augean Stables. In a stroke of brilliance, he diverted the close by rivers Alpheus and Peneus, channeling their robust currents through the stables. The forceful flow of water acted as a herbal cleaning agent, unexpectedly sweeping away the collected dust.

The efficiency of Heracles' plan was extremely good. In only a unmarried day, the Augean Stables have been transformed from a noxious and filthy surroundings right into a pristine and cleansed vicinity. The scale of this accomplishment changed into top notch and left witnesses, together with King Augeas, astonished at the hero's ingenuity.

However, the a achievement final touch of the exertions did not come with out its complications. King Augeas, likely taken aback via the use of the significance of Heracles' achievement, reneged on his promise to praise the hero. He claimed that Heracles had received divine assistance, predominant to a dispute among the 2.

Despite the dispute, Heracles' triumph in cleansing the Augean Stables showcased now not simplest his physical electricity however additionally his ability to leverage unconventional strategies and harness the forces of nature to overcome seemingly insurmountable traumatic conditions. This labor, marked through manner of its inventive method and the hero's energy of will, further solidified Heracles' recognition as a multifaceted hero endowed with electricity, intelligence, and hassle-solving capabilities.

6. Slaying the Stymphalian Birds

Heracles undertook the difficult responsibility of destroying the Stymphalian Birds, unstable monsters that haunted the marshes surrounding the city of Stymphalus, as one in each of his tough twelve labors. These significant birds were no longer ordinary adversaries; they possessed sharp metal feathers and a lethal functionality to shoot them as lethal projectiles.

The Stymphalian Birds posed a massive risk to the close by populace, wreaking havoc with their ferocious attacks. Heracles, tasked with bringing an forestall to their danger, approached the venture collectively together with his function mixture of power, approach, and divine help.

To conquer the Stymphalian Birds, Heracles sought the aid of the goddess Athena, who provided him with a completely unique and powerful weapon – a couple of bronze or copper cymbals. Forged by way of the use of the professional hands of Hephaestus, those cymbals had been designed to create a loud, clashing sound on the identical time as struck collectively, serving as a deterrent towards avian adversaries.

Heracles, armed with Athena's present, ventured into the marshes in which the Stymphalian Birds had taken house. Understanding the significance of adapting to the venture, he devised a technique that leveraged each his divine useful resource and his very very own archery competencies.

Employing the cymbals to create a cacophony of noise, Heracles startled and involved the Stymphalian Birds, forcing them to take flight. Seizing this opportunity, he skillfully used his bow and arrows to shoot down the birds one at a time. The assignment lay in the steel feathers that served as a herbal armor for the creatures, making traditional arrows vain.

However, Heracles' particular motive and strategic use of the cymbals allowed him to triumph over this obstacle. The loud noise created a disoriented and susceptible united states for the birds, permitting him to pierce via their defenses together with his arrows. The cease result became a successful battle that rid the vicinity of the Stymphalian Birds and ensured the protection of the community population.

The slaying of the Stymphalian Birds showcased Heracles' adaptability, resourcefulness, and willingness to are seeking out divine help even as confronted with particular traumatic situations. It underlined his dedication to protective the innocent and bringing peace to distressed lands, solidifying his popularity as a hero of unequalled prowess in Greek mythology.

7. Capture the Cretan Bull

Heracles faced the massive technique of taking pictures the Cretan Bull, a beast famed for its brilliant electricity and fury that end up wreaking devastation at the island of Crete, as one in each of his legendary twelve labors. Undeterred with the resource of the bull's reputation, Heracles launched proper right into a adventure to confront and subdue this effective adversary.

Upon arriving in Crete, Heracles faced the Cretan Bull in a fierce and hard war that examined his bodily prowess and braveness. With incredible strength and first rate bravery, he controlled to overpower the bull and efficaciously received manage over the strong creature.

Having subdued the Cretan Bull, Heracles lower lower back to King Eurystheus, supplying the bull as proof of his accomplishment. However, King Eurystheus, intimidated with the beneficial aid of the sheer energy of the bull, refused to simply accept it as a part of the finished exertions. Instead, he ordered Heracles to launch the bull again into the wild.

The launch of the Cretan Bull brought on unexpected results, because the powerful creature went at once to cause chaos and havoc in a single-of-a-kind areas, perpetuating the annoying conditions posed thru the creature. Eventually, the bull met its dying on the hands of every distinctive mythical hero, Theseus, at some point of his personal heroic adventures.

The seize of the Cretan Bull showcased Heracles' brilliant power, unwavering bravery, and potential to confront and overcome effective adversaries for the extra appropriate. While the final results of freeing the bull did not align with the preliminary reason of the hard work, the feat itself emphasised Heracles' indomitable spirit and his dedication to going via annoying conditions head-on. This tough paintings completed a essential characteristic in solidifying Heracles' recognition as a mythical hero in Greek mythology, celebrated for his high-quality feats of power and bravery.

eight. Steal the Mares of Diomedes

In a lesser-regarded but further wonderful tale, Heracles took on a in addition project outdoor of the valid twelve labors – the daunting mission of stealing the individual-

eating mares owned with the useful resource of King Diomedes of Thrace. These mythical horses had been notorious for their aggressive and uncontrollable behavior, as they were fed a weight loss plan of human flesh.

Undeterred by means of the usage of the unpleasant popularity of the mares, Heracles, discovered with the resource of his brave partners, embarked on a perilous challenge to the land of Diomedes. Upon venture their excursion spot, a fierce conflict ensued among Heracles and the king's guards, determined to protect the massive horses. Through sheer energy and strategic prowess, Heracles emerged a hit, overcoming the fierce resistance.

To appease and in the end control the violent nature of the man or woman-consuming mares, Heracles devised a formidable and unconventional answer. He fed them the flesh of their former draw close, King Diomedes himself. This formidable act now not most effective pacified the ferocious horses however also asserted Heracles' dominance over them, showcasing his resourcefulness in the face of apparently insurmountable disturbing conditions.

Having successfully tamed the mares, Heracles once more to King Eurystheus, supplying the ambitious creatures as tangible proof of his triumph over this greater labor. Although now not officially protected in the twelve assigned responsibilities, this feat underscored Heracles' exceptional braveness, physical power, and his capability to confront and subdue even the maximum bold and threatening adversaries.

This lesser-regarded myth contributes to the rich tapestry of Heracles' legendary exploits, highlighting his repute as a renowned hero in Greek mythology. It reinforces the issues of bravery, resourcefulness, and the hero's indomitable spirit which may be synonymous with the person of Heracles.

nine. Obtain the Belt of Hippolyta

One of the mythical labors assigned to Heracles become the difficult mission of obtaining the Belt of Hippolyta, the esteemed queen of the Amazons – a tribe renowned for its bold warrior ladies. The belt grow to be believed to very own wonderful energy, making it a coveted and symbolic artifact.

Undeterred with the beneficial resource of the bold reputation of the Amazons, Heracles released right into a journey to their land. His intention turn out to be first of all peaceful, searching for to negotiate with Hippolyta for the prized belt. Recognizing Heracles' mythical reputation and unmatched power, Hippolyta become inclined to offer his request as a gesture of goodwill.

However, the divine intervention of Hera, harboring her longstanding grudge in opposition to Heracles, brought a misleading twist to the narrative. Disguising herself as an Amazon, Hera spread malicious rumors the diverse tribe, falsely placing ahead that Heracles aimed to abduct their queen. As a result, the surroundings turned adverse, and what come to be purported to be a diplomatic come upon converted right right into a battlefield.

Faced with the enraged Amazons, Heracles found himself entangled in a fierce war of phrases. In the course of the warfare, he emerged a success, regardless of the truth that the versions of the parable range – a few recount Heracles slaying Hippolyta, at the identical time as others suggest he subdued her without inflicting her dying.

With the Belt of Hippolyta secured, Heracles departed from the Amazonian territory. Upon returning to King Eurystheus, he supplied the belt as tangible proof of his fulfillment in however a few one-of-a-kind difficult paintings. The acquisition of the belt now not only examined Heracles' formidable combat talents however additionally underscored his capability to conquer powerful adversaries.

However, the parable surrounding the Belt of Hippolyta moreover emphasised the disturbing conditions imposed upon Heracles via divine interference, in particular from Hera. The goddess's have an effect on, aimed closer to obstructing Heracles' improvement, introduced a layer of complexity to the hero's adventure, revealing the intricacies of the relationships among mortals and the gods in Greek mythology.

Ultimately, whilst the exertions involved conflict and bloodshed, it illuminated Heracles' unwavering perseverance and resolution in the face of adversity. The story in addition solidified his repute as a renowned hero capable of conducting apparently insurmountable obligations in the rich tapestry of Greek mythology.

10. Obtain the Cattle of the Monster Geryon

Getting the precious livestock that belonged to the terrifying Geryon grow to be one of the tough duties that Heracles turned into assigned. Geryon, a creature of fearsome repute, possessed three heads and our our bodies joined at the waist, showcasing each his big strength and the remarkable herd of impressive crimson livestock underneath his dominion.

Undaunted with the aid of the use of the traumatic conditions that lay in advance, Heracles launched into an arduous journey to the farthest reaches of the Western global, in which the island of Erytheia served as Geryon's living. The initial impediment in his route have grow to be the fierce parent dog Orthrus, a -headed hound, which Heracles valiantly confronted and successfully slew.

Having overcome Orthrus, Heracles confronted the tremendous Geryon himself in a conflict that echoed with depth. Despite Geryon's bold nature, Heracles employed his amazing combat capabilities to overpower the creature and emerge effective.

With Geryon defeated, Heracles claimed the prized crimson farm animals as his private. The next journey decrease returned to Greece, however, modified into now not with out more traumatic conditions. The solar god

Helios, angered with the aid of Heracles' movements, unleashed a swarm of biting flies to prevent his progress. Unfazed, Heracles verified his resourcefulness via the use of crafting a large bow, with which he skillfully shot down the difficult flies, safeguarding every himself and the precious livestock.

Upon achieving Greece, Heracles furnished the livestock of Geryon to King Eurystheus, thereby completing the difficult artwork. The king, astounded with the resource of the accomplishment and awestruck through the sight of the astounding pink cattle, bore witness to the success of but another terrific feat via the mythical hero.

The saga of obtaining Geryon's livestock underscored Heracles' amazing strength, unyielding bravery, and unrelenting perseverance. It served as a testomony to his capability to overcome bold adversaries and endure hardships at some point of his epic quests. This hard paintings in addition solidified Heracles' fame as a peerless hero, celebrated for his fantastic feats within the wealthy tapestry of Greek fantasy.

11. Steal the Apples of the Hesperides

The ambitious mission to remove the Apples of the Hesperides—favored golden apples with the legendary capacity to supply immortality—turned into one in all Heracles' herculean labors. Undertaking this hard challenge, Heracles launched into a journey that could test no longer only his power but also his mind and resourcefulness.

In his pursuit of the Apples of the Hesperides, Heracles sought the help of the Titan Atlas. Atlas, pressured with the responsibility of helping the heavens, have emerge as a important superb friend in this quest. Heracles cleverly negotiated with Atlas, convincing him to retrieve the apples while he shouldered the load of the heavens in Atlas's stead.

As Atlas launched into the task, there has been a realistic twist to the affiliation. Aware that Atlas might not willingly resume his burden, Heracles proposed a short transfer, all through which Atlas also can want to in short reclaim the heavens. This allowed Heracles to better function himself and, seizing the opportune 2d, hold close the Apples of the Hesperides.

With the golden apples in his possession, Heracles left Atlas to undergo the celestial weight all another time, securing his escape. The hero, now in possession of the coveted fruits, made his manner returned to King Eurystheus, determined to provide him with the wonderful spoils of his tough work.

Upon his go back, Heracles unveiled the Apples of the Hesperides to King Eurystheus, signifying the crowning glory of but each other remarkable mission. The king, astounded with the aid of the hero's ingenuity and fulfillment, bore witness to the tangible proof of Heracles' unheard of talents.

The theft of the Apples of the Hesperides showcased now not most effective Heracles' physical prowess however additionally his foxy and strategic thinking. It discovered out his capability to navigate complex conditions and outsmart effective beings to gather his goals. Moreover, the tough artwork underscored the mythical importance of the golden apples, symbolizing immortality and divine overall performance.

Heracles' a fulfillment acquisition of those mythical apples further solidified his fame as a hero of splendid stature, capable of undertaking and triumphing over exquisite stressful situations in the rich tapestry of Greek mythology.

12. Capture Cerberus

In the end result of his legendary labors, Heracles faced the ambitious project of taking pictures Cerberus, the ferocious three-headed hound guarding the entrance to the Underworld in Greek mythology. This Herculean challenge now not excellent showcased his unequalled energy but additionally examined his potential to navigate the geographical regions of the divine and emerge a success in opposition to the most fearsome adversaries.

To provoke this perilous quest, Heracles first ventured to Eleusis, in which he underwent the sacred initiation rites of the Eleusinian Mysteries. By gaining the decide on of the goddess Demeter thru those rituals, Heracles secured divine steerage for his drawing near venture – a adventure into the depths of the Underworld to seize the scary Cerberus.

Setting forth toward the gates of the Underworld, Heracles sought permission from Hades, the ruler of the sector of the useless. Hades granted acclaim for Heracles to capture Cerberus but imposed a difficult situation – the hero want to subdue the excellent dog with out using any guns.

Undeterred by means of the usage of way of the daunting situations, Heracles descended into the abyss, armed remarkable alongside together with his naked arms and indomitable power. Confronting Cerberus at the gates, a fierce and tumultuous war ensued. Despite the hound's 3 menacing heads and ferocious demeanor, Heracles, with sheer might possibly and resolution, controlled to overpower Cerberus and gain manage over the fearsome determine.

With Cerberus now under his command, Heracles ascended from the depths of the Underworld to the ground international. Along the manner, he encountered severa barriers, in conjunction with the mystical river Styx and the goddess Persephone, however his excellent prowess allowed him to navigate the ones demanding situations efficiently.

Upon returning to King Eurystheus, Heracles provided Cerberus as tangible proof of his overcome the ambitious creature. The sight of the terrifying three-headed canine struck terror into the heart of the king, who changed into now witness to the indomitable energy and braveness of Heracles.

The capture of Cerberus stood as a testament to Heracles' brilliant skills and his willingness to face unimaginable demanding situations. By venturing into the sacred and perilous nation-states of the Underworld, Heracles no longer tremendous fulfilled the tough responsibilities assigned to him but also solidified his fame as a hero capable of confronting the divine and growing a success in opposition to the most formidable combatants.

Chapter 4: Monsters And Creatures In Greek Myth

Greek mythology, a realm teeming with gods, heroes, and epic quests, is similarly famend for its pantheon of monsters and creatures. These fantastical beings, born from the chaos of primordial lifestyles, add a layer of awe, worry, and fascination to the difficult tapestry of Greek fantasy. From multi-headed hydras to foxy sphinxes, the spectrum of monsters in Greek mythology is as various as it is legendary. These monsters and creatures, embodiments of chaos, future, and divine punishment, characteristic bold adversaries for heroes and testaments to the boundless creativeness of historic Greek writers. Each one contributes to the tricky ethical and metaphysical landscape of Greek fable.

The Hydra: A Mythical Serpent

Within the huge material of Greek mythology, the Hydra stands as a fearsome and iconic creature, a serpent-like being with regenerative powers that struck terror into the hearts of ancient storytellers and heroes alike. This large entity, living close to the town of Lerna in treacherous swamps, have grow to be a photo of indomitable mission and the embodiment of patience inside the face of adversity.

According to the historical stories, the Hydra changed into born of the union among Typhon and Echidna, primordial beings with huge traits. The Hydra's lair, the swamps of Lerna, delivered an air of thriller of mystery and chance to its lifestyles. Most significantly, this creature possessed an remarkable characteristic – a couple of heads, the high-quality amount of which various in fantastic debts, with one head taken into consideration immortal.

The Hydra's maximum ambitious element lay in its capability to regenerate heads. Each time a head modified into severed, extra may boom in its place. This regenerative energy, coupled with its poisonous blood, made the Hydra an insurmountable undertaking for any who dared to face it.

The mythical come across between Hercules and the Hydra have emerge as a critical narrative in Greek mythology. Hercules, in atonement for the tragic insanity that added about the killing of his partner and children, come to be assigned the Twelve Labors, with the defeat of the Hydra being one of the maximum daunting responsibilities.

The conflict between Hercules and the Hydra end up a testomony to the hero's power, resourcefulness, and strategic prowess. Armed with a sword and a flaming torch, Hercules devised a manner to overcome the

Hydra's regenerative ability. After decapitating a head, he used the torch to cauterize the stump, stopping new heads from sprouting. In this epic war, Hercules received essential useful resource from his nephew Iolaus, who achieved a pivotal function in making sure the fulfillment of the challenge.

The Hydra's symbolism extends beyond its legendary lifestyles. It represents the perennial stressful conditions in existence – the ones continual and tenacious limitations that seem to broaden back on every occasion they may be confronted. Hercules' victory over the Hydra serves as a metaphorical lesson, emphasizing the necessity of managing and overcoming reputedly insurmountable troubles, notwithstanding the fact that they constantly reappear.

In cutting-edge tradition, the Hydra has turn out to be a powerful photograph, regularly hired to represent multifaceted issues or threats that constantly resurface. Its presence in Greek mythology contributes to the wealthy and diverse array of creatures and monsters that populate the historical stories, inclusive of depth and complexity to the iconic legacy of these captivating myths. The Hydra stays an extended lasting brand of the indomitable spirit required to confront existence's disturbing conditions head-on, irrespective of how formidable they may seem.

The Chimera and the Sphinx: Mythical Beasts

Two legendary creatures stand as iconic symbols of ferocity, enigma, and the triumph of heroic endeavors – the Chimera and the Sphinx. These legendary beings, born of primordial unions, encompass the demanding situations that heroes ought to face, showcasing the need for courage, wit, and strategic prowess to triumph over reputedly insurmountable odds.

The Chimera, a creature of nightmarish visage, modified into stated to be the offspring of Typhon and Echidna, rising inside the vicinity of Lycia in Asia Minor. With the frame and head of a lion, a goat's head sticking out from its once more, and a serpent's tail, the Chimera struck fear into the hearts of all who beheld it. Its fiery breath and damaging nature terrorized the land, devouring each cattle and human beings.

The hero Bellerophon, aided via the use of the winged horse Pegasus, took up the mantle of managing the Chimera. In a dramatic aerial confrontation, Bellerophon thrust a lead-tipped spear into the creature's fiery maw, slicing off its breath and bringing an end to its reign of terror. The Chimera's defeat symbolizes the triumph of human ingenuity and valor over big threats, illustrating the heroic archetype's functionality to confront and triumph over formidable foes.

The Sphinx, with its enigmatic nature and affiliation with riddles, offers a completely unique form of venture. Sent with the aid of manner of the gods as a punishment to the town of Thebes, the Sphinx need to pose a riddle to passersby. Failure to reply correctly resulted within the Sphinx devouring the unlucky soul. The riddle, famously solved via Oedipus, asked approximately a creature strolling on 4 legs inside the morning, legs at noon, and three legs in the middle of the night, with the solution being a human.

Oedipus, demonstrating thoughts and know-how, efficiently replied the Sphinx's riddle, main to the creature's demise. The Sphinx, defeated and humiliated, threw itself off a cliff, ending its tyrannical rule over Thebes. This story serves as a testomony to the strength of mind and hassle-solving in the face of intellectual demanding situations, showcasing the triumph of data over adversity.

Both the Chimera and the Sphinx, with their fantastic dispositions and symbolic significance, have left an indelible mark on Greek mythology. These legendary creatures maintain to captivate and encourage, serving as effective metaphors for the long-lasting human warfare in competition to superb forces and the triumph of heroes who dare to stand them head-on. Their recollections resonate thru the a long time, reminding us of the timeless difficulty subjects of courage, wit, and the indomitable spirit of folks who confront the mythical challenges that rise up within the human enjoy.

The Centaurs: Bridging the Divide Between Human and Beast

In the complex Greek myths, the Centaur emerges as a fascinating and complicated creature, embodying the fusion of human thoughts and untamed herbal dispositions. With its remarkable shape – the higher frame and head of a human seamlessly melded with the powerful decrease body of a horse – the Centaur occupies a unique area within the mythological landscape, symbolizing the interaction among civilization and the desert.

The Centaurs were believed to be the descendants of Ixion, a mortal king, and Nephele, a cloud nymph. Renowned for his or her untamed and frequently rowdy nature, Centaurs were related to excesses, mainly in the nation-states of drunkenness and violence. Their chaotic behavior regularly introduced approximately conflicts and clashes, portraying them as formidable however unpredictable beings.

Among the pantheon of Centaurs, one determine stands out in stark evaluation – Chiron. Unlike his unruly contrary numbers, Chiron have become characterized by way of information, kindness, and a unique skills in medicine and the arts. Serving as a mentor to legendary heroes together with Achilles and Jason, Chiron challenged the stereotype of Centaurs, showcasing a nuanced and multifaceted portrayal of those mythical beings.

Centaurs often made appearances in Greek myths, frequently depicted as fierce warriors taking component in battles and conflicts. Their twin nature, straddling the geographical regions of humanity and the untamed desert, served as a symbolic instance of the everlasting conflict among civilization and primal instincts. This tension maximum of the human and the bestial indoors Centaurs mirrors the complexities inherent in human nature itself.

The Centaur serves as a effective metaphor for the blending of human and animal abilities, illustrating the tough interaction among cause and instinct. This mythical creature encapsulates the continuing internal battle internal people, reflecting the perennial tension among the civilized thoughts and the untamed barren location that is living within.

Beyond the geographical regions of mythology, the Centaur has transcended its origins to grow to be a high-quality determine in artwork, literature, and popular way of existence. The enduring fascination with Centaurs lies of their ability to seize the creativeness, inviting contemplation on the sensitive equilibrium amongst human mind and the primal forces that form our lifestyles. As a photo of the complex relationship among humanity and the natural global, the Centaur keeps to inspire and initiate belief, remaining a undying and enigmatic presence inside the vast realm of delusion and storytelling.

The Harpies: Winged Enforcers of Divine Retribution

The Harpies turn out to be ambitious and enigmatic creatures, embodying the relentless forces of typhoon winds and turning in rapid retribution. With their setting look – a aggregate of a girl's face seamlessly included with the body of a fowl – the Harpies symbolize the ominous messengers of doom and outlets of divine justice.

The portrayal of Harpies in Greek mythology is constant in their function as harbingers of doom and fast punishers of wrongdoing. Often dispatched via the gods to execute divine justice, Harpies are famend for his or her ruthless efficiency in wearing out their appointed duties. Their functionality to grab away transgressors and deliver them to face divine retribution establishes them as effective enforcers of cosmic order.

The particular appearance of the Harpies, combining the airy splendor of a female with the predatory shape of a chook, presents an element of mystique and terror to their man or woman. This amalgamation of human and avian attributes serves as a visible instance of the legendary realm's boundless creativity and the transcendence of conventional paperwork.

One tremendous detail of the Harpies' feature is their affiliation with hurricane winds. This connection underscores their elemental nature, highlighting their ability to harness the forces of nature to mete out punishment. The winds, frequently symbolic of exchange and upheaval, align with the transformative and frequently irreversible results of divine justice.

While the Harpies' appearances in numerous myths are brief, their effect is profound. One well-known stumble upon takes place inside the tale of the Argonauts, where the Harpies torment the blind seer Phineas, snatching away his meals and rendering it inedible. This act of torment symbolizes the disruptive and chaotic nature of divine intervention, emphasizing the unpredictability of future.

The Harpies, with their relentless pursuit of justice, cross beyond their roles as mere legendary entities. They turn out to be symbolic representations of the consequences of 1's movements and the inevitability of going through divine retribution. The Harpies feature a cautionary element inside the difficult moral framework of Greek mythology, underscoring the belief in a cosmic order that needs stability and justice.

In the broader cultural context, the Harpies hold to captivate audiences with their mysterious and ambitious presence. Their portrayal as avian entities with a awesome human countenance has stimulated innovative interpretations, literature, and cultural references, solidifying their popularity as enduring symbols of divine effect. As winged enforcers of justice, the Harpies stand as a testament to the long-lasting energy of myth to maintain complicated moral and cosmic truths at some stage in generations.

Gorgons: The Terrifying Sisters of Stone

In the pantheon, the Gorgons grow to be a trio of vast sisters, with Medusa recognition due to the fact the most infamous among them. These terrifying beings, characterised with the aid of using their serpentine locks and the petrifying energy in their gaze, encompass a effective mixture of horror and mythic intrigue.

The Gorgons have been born from the union of Typhon and Echidna, two primordial beings stated for spawning numerous large creatures. The sisters – Medusa, Stheno, and Euryale – shared a commonplace trait that rendered them notorious and feared: snakes for hair and a gaze that have become folks who met it into stone.

While all 3 Gorgons were formidable, Medusa's call has transcended the mythic realm to turn out to be synonymous with this giant trio. Her tale took a dramatic turn at the same time as the hero Perseus, aided thru the usage of divine gadgets, launched proper into a quest to slay Medusa and claim her head as a trophy. The decapitation of Medusa, a feat that required strategic cunning and divine help, brought forth large beings – the winged horse Pegasus and the large Chrysaor.

The defining feature of the Gorgons modified into their capability to reveal onlookers to stone with a single look. This petrifying gaze brought an element of horror to their mythology, growing an air of mystery of hazard and doom that surrounded those significant sisters. The notion of assembly the eyes of a Gorgon carried with it the burden of an irreversible and terrifying future.

Medusa's decapitation no longer great resulted within the birth of mythical creatures however additionally solidified her legacy as a symbol of triumph over huge adversity. Her severed head, used as a weapon via the use of the use of Perseus and later talented to the goddess Athena, became a sturdy talisman with the electricity to repel foes.

The Gorgons, specifically Medusa, have transcended their mythic origins to become symbolic figures in art. Medusa, mainly, is frequently portrayed as a complicated photo – from a big chance to a illustration of lady power and defiance. The Gorgons, with their serpentine visages and petrifying gazes, occupy a very specific and enduring vicinity within the tapestry of Greek mythology. Their stories evoke a sense of every fear and fascination, portraying them as mythical beings with the electricity to convert the very nature of those who stumble upon them. Medusa, due to the fact the maximum famend Gorgon, stands as a testament to the complicated interaction of horror, triumph, and symbolism within the realm of ancient Greek myths.

The Minotaur: Labyrinthine Horror

In the labyrinthine depths of Greek fable, the Minotaur stands as a creature every large and tragic, born from an unnatural union and destined for a dark future. The narrative surrounding the Minotaur weaves collectively issues of forbidden love, complicated mazes, and the heroism of those who dare to confront the beast.

The Minotaur's origins lie inside the ill-fated union amongst Queen Pasiphae and a bull, a union facilitated thru the usage of the god Poseidon's divine intervention or punishment. From this unnatural coupling emerged a creature with the body of a person and the top of a bull – the Minotaur. This hybrid being, cursed from its inception, found its dwelling inside the labyrinth crafted thru the modern Daedalus at the island of Crete.

Commissioned with the aid of manner of King Minos, the labyrinth have become the Minotaur's prison and the stage for a ugly tribute demanded from Athens. Every nine years, seven younger men and seven maidens had been sent as tributes to Crete, destined to face the Minotaur's voracious urge for food. The labyrinth's complexity ensured that those who entered need to never locate their manner out.

Enter Theseus, the valiant hero of Athens, who volunteered to be one of the tributes with the rationale to slay the Minotaur and stop the grisly cycle. Aided through way of the use of Ariadne, the daughter of King Minos, Theseus acquired a thread that might function his lifeline in navigating the labyrinth. Armed with courage and determination, he ventured into the maze to confront the Minotaur.

Ariadne's thread proved instrumental in Theseus' quest, allowing him to navigate the labyrinth's elaborate passages and retrace his steps after defeating the Minotaur. The symbolic significance of the thread extends beyond its sensible use, representing the interaction of destiny, preference, and the guiding force of companionship.

The climactic come across amongst Theseus and the Minotaur unfold out within the labyrinth's oppressive walls. Armed with a sword and guided via manner of Ariadne's thread, Theseus confronted the creature in mortal fight. In a 2nd of heroism, Theseus slew the Minotaur, bringing an prevent to the beast's reign of terror and the gruesome tributes from Athens.

The Minotaur's tale includes an inherent tragedy – a creature born of unnatural activities and condemned to a life of huge existence within the labyrinth. Its future, original via the choices of others, culminated in a heroic warfare of terms that, at the same time as liberating Athens from the tributes, did little to regulate the Minotaur's predetermined destiny.

The Minotaur's labyrinthine lair and its remaining defeat have permeated Western literature, art work, and philosophy, serving as a metaphor for navigating the complexities of lifestyles and overcoming inner demons. The Minotaur stands as a image of the large outcomes that can stand up from the interaction of divine intervention, human folly, and the inescapable labyrinth of fate. The Minotaur, with its enigmatic origins and labyrinth-high-quality life, embodies the tragic and fantastical factors of Greek mythology. Its tale, interwoven with problems of heroism, forbidden love, and the look for liberation, maintains to captivate imaginations, reminding us of the iconic electricity of delusion to discover the depths of the human enjoy.

Cyclopes: Forgers of Thunder

The Cyclopes come to be bold one-eyed giants, no longer merely creatures of brute electricity, but professional blacksmiths endowed with a unique connection to thunder and lightning. Among those Cyclopes, the maximum renowned is Polyphemus, whose story intertwines with the epic adventure of Odysseus in Homer's immortal adventure.

The Cyclopes, a race of large beings, have been stated to inhabit the a long way off corners of the vicinity. Known for his or her solitary eye, large energy, and know-how in craftsmanship, they executed a pivotal characteristic inside the divine realm. The maximum exquisite amongst them were Brontes, Steropes, and Arges, who've been credited with forging the powerful thunderbolts wielded by using Zeus.

The association of Cyclopes with thunder and lightning highlighted their crucial role within the divine armory. In the depths in their mythical forges, those one-eyed giants crafted the powerful thunderbolts that Zeus, the king of the gods, would possibly hire to show up his divine wrath. This connection stepped forward the Cyclopes past mere giants, casting them as important participants to the cosmic stability.

Polyphemus, a Cyclops and son of Poseidon takes center degree in the Odyssey, Homer's epic saga of Odysseus' onerous adventure home after the Trojan War. Odysseus and his guys, sailing the seas, stumbled upon the island of the Cyclops, in which they encountered the large and voracious Polyphemus.

Odysseus, famend for his cunning, devised a plan to escape Polyphemus' clutches. He provided the Cyclops a sturdy wine, claiming it as a gesture of goodwill. When Polyphemus succumbed to the results of the wine, Odysseus and his men exploited the opportunity. They drove a sharpened stake into the Cyclops' unmarried eye, rendering him blind and inclined.

Polyphemus, robbed of his sight, bellowed in ache and sought vengeance upon Odysseus. The hero's cleverness, however, allows him to get away the Cyclops' lair with the useful resource of manner of tying his men beneath Polyphemus' sheep, evading the big's wrath and making sure their persisted journey.

The Cyclopes, with their legendary prowess in forging thunderbolts and their memorable encounters with legendary heroes, left an indelible mark on Greek mythology. Their affiliation with elemental forces, craftsmanship, and epic memories underscores their importance within the broader tapestry of ancient Greek storytelling.

Beyond their bodily prowess and mythic exploits, the Cyclopes symbolize more than mere giants. Their solitary eye represents a completely precise attitude – an notion into craftsmanship, elemental forces, and the cyclical nature of divine retribution. Polyphemus' blinding serves as a metaphor for the consequences of hubris, showcasing the touchy balance amongst cunning and divine wrath.

Chapter 5: The Underworld And The Afterlife

Hades: Guardians of the Afterlife

In this section, we narrate how Hades emerges as a essential decide, presiding over the mysterious and enigmatic realm of the Underworld. As the god chargeable for the souls of the departed, Hades, brother to Zeus and Poseidon, governs the unseen realm in which the solar sun shades of the deceased discover their everlasting abode.

In the divine hierarchy, Hades, along Zeus and Poseidon, paperwork the triumvirate that governs the cosmos. While Zeus reigns over the skies and Earth, and Poseidon commands the seas, Hades holds dominion over the place of the dead. Together, they hold a touchy balance that mirrors the interconnectedness of life, dying, and the everlasting.

The Underworld, synonymous with every the god Hades and the area itself, unfolds as a complicated expanse with brilliant regions.

Among the ones, the Fields of Asphodel stand as a somber homestead for the souls of everyday mortals, their lifestyles with out notable joy or sorrow. In stark assessment, the Elysian Fields offer a paradisiacal haven reserved for the heroic and virtuous souls, a praise for a lifestyles properly-lived.

Yet, inside the Underworld's depths lies Tartarus, an abyss of everlasting torment. Here, the maximum malevolent souls or perhaps the formidable Titans discover themselves imprisoned, a testomony to Hades' function as every determine and jailer.

Depicted as a determine of solemnity and gravitas, Hades is often shrouded in darkness, mirroring the person of his dominion. A darkish cloak drapes his shape, and in his hand, he wields a wand or key, symbolizing his authority over the gates of the Underworld. While mortals may worry him, Hades does no longer personify evil but alternatively serves due to the fact the vigilant custodian of the afterlife.

Hades' presence extends beyond his feature as a ruler. One of the most renowned myths surrounding Hades is his abduction of Persephone, daughter of Demeter, to become his queen within the Underworld. This union is intrinsically related to the converting seasons on Earth, revealing the god's tough involvement in the herbal order.

In the parable of Orpheus and Eurydice, Hades assumes a pivotal function while Orpheus descends into the Underworld to retrieve his liked accomplice. This narrative underscores Hades' adherence to the laws of the afterlife and the traumatic situations faced via the use of individuals who dare to defy its order.

The concept of the Underworld, and via the use of extension, Hades, profoundly inspired Greek tradition. Elaborate funeral rites and rituals have been performed to appease the gods and ensure a secure passage for the departed. The Underworld's portrayal shows the Greeks' acknowledgment of the ephemeral nature of life and the inexorable march in the route of loss of life.

In summary, Hades and the Underworld represent not tremendous the inevitable excursion spot of all mortal souls but moreover the embodiment of cosmic stability and justice. The god Hades, together along with his stern countenance, stands as a sentinel, overseeing the perpetual cycle of life, loss of life, and the mysteries that lie beyond the edge of mortal existence.

The River Styx and the Ferryman, Charon: Navigating the Boundaries of the Afterlife

The River Styx and the enigmatic ferryman, Charon, stand as iconic symbols, marking the airy boundary many of the land of the residing and the region of the useless.

The River Styx, a darkish and mysterious watercourse that meanders via the Underworld, is more than a trifling river—it's far a liminal region with profound implications for each mortals and immortals. It serves as a boundary, a symbolic threshold that delineates the transition from existence to death. The Styx is often portrayed as a somber and formidable body of water, casting an enforcing silhouette at the psyche of individuals who navigate its currents.

Beyond its geographical presence, the River Styx is invested with magical homes, gambling a pivotal role inside the rituals and myths of historical Greece. It modified into taken into consideration to have an oath-binding satisfactory and solemn pledges made with the aid of the gods were often sworn upon its sacred waters. This mystical aspect advanced the Styx to a realm of cosmic significance, intertwining its currents with the very cloth of divine governance.

For souls transitioning to the afterlife, the River Styx represented a essential passage. In Greek mythology, the deceased were obligated to traverse its dark expanse, guided with the resource of rituals and divine interventions. The river have become a image of transition and purification, reflecting the profound belief within the significance of proper burial rites and the sanctity of the journey into the afterlife.

The River Styx served as a conduit for divine justice. It have emerge as entwined with the administering of oaths maximum of the gods, emphasizing the gravity of ensures made in its name. The river moreover finished a role in purification rituals and served as a backdrop for divine punishments, reinforcing its twin nature as each a mystical pressure and an arbiter of cosmic order.

Inextricably associated with the River Styx is Charon, the aged ferryman who plies the Stygian waters, orchestrating the passage of souls the diverse worlds. Charon assumes the pivotal characteristic of escorting the deceased throughout the river into the depths of the Underworld.

Charon is depicted as a grizzled determine, his lengthy beard testifying to the eons he has spent due to the fact the figure of the crossing. His boat, a vessel poised among geographical regions, will become the conduit for the souls of the departed, mirroring the existential journey from existence's seashores to the obsidian depths of Hades.

The mythos surrounding Charon contain a toll for his offerings. To make sure a constant passage, the deceased were buried with a coin or an obol under their tongues. This symbolic charge underscored the historical notion inside the importance of financial transactions even within the afterlife and manifested the difficult relationship many of the living and the arena of the vain.

The River Styx and Charon encompass profound symbolism. Together, they constitute the delicate stability amongst lifestyles and loss of life, the brink that all must float. The rituals, ideals, and mythic narratives surrounding the ones entities echo the deep cultural reverence that the historic Greeks held for the transition from mortal existence to the afterlife.

The River Styx and Charon end up metaphysical guardians, navigating the touchy intersection a number of the ephemeral realm of the living and the shadowy expanses of the Underworld. They encapsulate the intricacies of historical ideals, wherein oaths held the load of cosmic order, and the transition from existence to dying modified right into a sacred adventure guided via the currents of the mystical Styx.

The Judges of the Dead: Arbiters of Fate inside the Underworld

The adventure of the soul did now not stop with the crossing of the River Styx and the guidance of Charon. Beyond the Stygian waters lay the world of judgment, presided over through the ambitious Judges of the Dead—Rhadamanthus, Minos, and Aeacus. These respected deities assumed the weighty obligation of figuring out the eternal destiny of departed souls.

Chapter 6: Love, Sexuality, And Family
Aphrodite And Eros

Aphrodite: Goddess of Love, Beauty, and Desire

In the expansive pantheon of Greek deities, Aphrodite emerges because the embodiment of affection, beauty, and fertility, fascinating each gods and mortals in conjunction with her now not feasible to face up to attraction. According to myth, her beginning is as fascinating as her personality—born from the sea foam close to Cyprus after the castration of Uranus. This goddess of affection wields the electricity to encourage choice and affection, her radiance echoing inside the geographical areas of divine and mortal hearts alike.

Aphrodite's myths are woven with romantic entanglements that pass beyond the bounds of the mortal and divine. Among her recollections, the narrative of the Trojan War stands prominently. In a opposition of beauty, she promised Paris, a Trojan prince, the affection of the most stunning mortal, Helen. This promise, fulfilled with the kidnapping of Helen, catalyzed the mythical struggle of the Trojan War, revealing the strong affect of affection at the affairs of gods and men.

Eros, the son of Aphrodite, takes center degree due to the fact the mischievous and playful god of affection and choice. Often portrayed as a more youthful winged boy armed with bow and arrows, Eros's whimsical antics shape the destinies of these touched thru his enchanted arrows, weaving threads of love and passion.

One of the maximum celebrated myths regarding Eros unfolds inside the love story of Eros and Psyche. Psyche, a mortal princess of exceptional splendor, unwittingly will become the target of Aphrodite's envy. In a bid to thwart Psyche's beauty from overshadowing her personal, Aphrodite obligations Eros with making Psyche fall in love with a hideous creature. Yet, Eros himself succumbs to like's enchantment, installing movement a tale of trials and tribulations that culminate inside the reunion of the 2 fans.

The myths of Aphrodite and Eros delve into the elaborate tapestry of affection, desire, and beauty. They navigate subjects of jealousy, energy dynamics, and the multifaceted nature of romantic relationships. Through those myths, the historic Greeks sought to clear up the complexities of human emotions, celebrating the joyous highs and acknowledging the tumultuous lows inherent within the realm of affection.

Aphrodite and Eros, via their timeless myths, transcend the limits of mythological narratives, turning into archetypes that resonate with the eternal dance of affection and preference. These tales no longer only do away with darkness from the divine influences on mortal affairs however moreover serve as poignant reflections on the human revel in of affection—a pressure each enthralling and capricious, capable of shaping destinies and steerage the direction of epic memories

The Relationship Between Zeus and Hera

The union among Zeus and Hera, because of the fact the king and queen of the Olympian gods, stands as a testament to the problematic dynamics interior divine relationships. While their divine recognition offers them huge energy and authority, their marriage is a long way from a harmonious and idyllic partnership.

Zeus, the king of the gods, commands the place of the sky and thunder, symbolizing perfect authority. However, his regal stature is followed via a proclivity for extramarital affairs and love entanglements. Despite his position due to the reality the ruler of Mount Olympus, Zeus' dalliances with each goddesses and mortal ladies upload a layer of complexity to his relationship with Hera.

Hera, due to the fact the goddess of marriage and circle of relatives, occupies a role intrinsically tied to the sanctity of matrimony. Her character is described with the aid of using a fierce protectiveness over her function as Zeus' partner. Hera is portrayed as a deity fueled via jealousy and vengefulness, directed now not terrific towards her philandering husband however additionally closer to his severa fanatics and their offspring.

The relationship amongst Zeus and Hera is riddled with conflicts and times of divine retribution. Hera's wrath regularly descends upon Zeus' mistresses and illegitimate kids, her jealousy transforming into vindictive actions. These tumultuous encounters end up the backdrop of many epic tales, showcasing the annoying situations confronted with the beneficial aid of a divine couple grappling with troubles of fidelity and betrayal.

At its middle, the connection amongst Zeus and Hera serves as a microcosm of the broader issues of marriage, electricity dynamics, and loyalty. Their divine recognition does not exempt them from going thru worrying conditions that reflect the ones encountered with the aid of using mortal couples. The myths surrounding Zeus and Hera delve into the intricacies of lengthy-term relationships, exploring fidelity, jealousy, and the enduring struggles which could outline such unions.

Despite the conflicts and Zeus' infidelity, the divine couple is not with out moments of crew spirit. Certain myths painting Zeus and Hera as allies, setting apart their versions to shield Olympus in competition to outside threats. This dual nature of their courting emphasizes that, no matter their discord, they percentage a mutual hobby in stabilizing and preserving their divine realm.

The courting among Zeus and Hera epitomizes the complex interaction among divine personalities. It weaves a tale of love, betrayal, and the traumatic situations inherent in retaining a protracted lasting union, even inside the lofty geographical regions of Mount Olympus. Through their myths, Zeus and Hera grow to be archetypes embodying the intricacies of marital dynamics, wherein divine authority and celestial strength do not shield them from the poignant trials that outline the essence of their divine partnership.

Demeter and Persephone: The Eternal Dance of Seasons

The tale of Demeter and Persephone unfolds in the nation-states of fertility, agriculture, and the perpetual cycle of existence and lack of existence. Demeter, the nurturing goddess of abundance and the harvest presides over the Earth's bounties, making sure the flourishing of plants and the prosperity of the land.

Persephone, the daughter of Demeter, embodies splendor and innocence. Her presence symbolizes the power of spring and the colorful shades that emerge with the converting seasons. However, her destiny becomes entwined with the Underworld even as Hades, captivated via her appeal, makes a decision to make her his queen.

The narrative takes a poignant flip as Hades abducts Persephone, spiriting her away to the depths of the Underworld. Demeter, devastated by using manner of the lack of her cherished daughter, plunges the sector right proper into a nation of desolation. The as soon as-fertile fields wither, and a perpetual wintry climate descends, mirroring the goddess's inconsolable grief.

Zeus, witnessing the discomfort of the Earth and its population, intervenes to negotiate Persephone's launch. A compromise is reached, but the wily Hades recommendations Persephone into eating pomegranate seeds, binding her to the Underworld. A bittersweet settlement is cast – Persephone will spend part of the one year inside the Underworld and part on Earth.

This arrangement lays the muse for the cyclical nature of seasons. When Persephone is living in the Underworld, Demeter mourns her absence, and the Earth languishes in barren coldness, embodying the harshness of winter. Conversely, whilst mom and daughter reunite, Demeter rejoices, and the Earth blossoms into a colourful life, ushering in spring and summer time.

At its center, the parable delves into profound problems of motherhood, loss, and the eternal cycle of renewal. Demeter's grief shows the conventional ache of a mom separated from her infant, on the identical time as Persephone's dual existence mirrors the tough dance between existence and demise.

The tale of Demeter and Persephone underscores the interaction among the divine and mortal geographical regions. It no longer best explains the changing seasons but moreover serves as a metaphor for the interconnectedness of the gods with the mortal international. The emotions of the deities right away have an impact at the Earth, demonstrating the intimate relationship between the divine and the terrestrial.

The enduring delusion of Demeter and Persephone stands as a timeless allegory, weaving collectively the threads of nature's rhythms, maternal love, and the inevitable passage of existence into loss of lifestyles and rebirth. The eternal dance of the goddesses continues to echo through the converting seasons, reminding humanity of the interconnected tapestry of existence and the profound impact of each grief and delight on the place spherical us.

Chapter 7: Influence Of Greek Myth In Art And Literature

The Renaissance, a period marked with the aid of using a revival of classical studying and a profound hobby in the innovative achievements of historical Greece, determined its muse in the wealthy tapestry of Greek mythology. This resurgence had a profound impact on the issue topics, topics, and varieties of Renaissance paintings, sculpting a cultural and aesthetic panorama that echoed the grandeur of classical antiquity.

Revival of Classical Mythology in Art

Mythological Narratives as Symbolic Exploration: One of the most placing strategies Greek mythology stimulated Renaissance artwork changed into thru the resurgence of classical mythology as a primary scenario depend. Artists, stimulated through the usage of the myths and tales of historic Greece, observed in the ones narratives a canvas to find out human emotions, virtues, and vices symbolically and metaphorically.

Gods and Goddesses as Artistic Subjects: Greek gods and goddesses took center stage as famous topics for Renaissance artists. Paintings and sculptures depicted the ones divine figures in idealized human forms, embellished with symbols representing their mythological roles. This portrayal sought to capture the splendor, grace, and electricity attributed to those deities, aligning with the Renaissance birthday party of ideals like harmony and balance.

Technical Mastery and Artistic Expression

Showcasing Artistic Prowess: The narratives of Greek mythology have grow to be a playground for artists to show off their technical capabilities and mastery of severa artistic factors. From anatomy to composition and attitude, artists proven their abilties through the example of complicated mythological memories, dramatic poses, and dynamic gestures.

Influence Beyond the Canvas: Literature, Theater, and Opera

Adaptation and Reinterpretation: Greek mythology not best discovered its vicinity in visible arts but moreover left its indelible mark on literature, theater, and opera at some stage in the Renaissance. These creative paperwork tailored and reinterpreted the myths for modern-day-day audiences, making use of the memories of gods and heroes to find out the moral, philosophical, and social thoughts of the time.

Architectural Aesthetics and Beyond

Architectural Incorporation: The impact of Greek mythology transcended person creative endeavors, shaping the very aesthetic of the Renaissance. Elements of classical Greek shape, together with columns, pediments, and proportions, located their manner into Renaissance homes and sculptures, growing a harmonious aggregate of classical beliefs and Renaissance innovation.

Cultural Heritage

Connecting with Cultural Heritage: Greek mythology provided Renaissance artists with a profound connection to the cultural heritage of historical Greece. It allowed them to delve into timeless human reports, developing enduring works of art work that served as a bridge among the classical beyond and the evolving Renaissance era.

The have an impact on of Greek mythology on Renaissance art work have emerge as a transformative stress that formed the modern panorama of the period. It now not best furnished artists with captivating tales and characters but moreover have become a vessel for exploring the complexities of the human situation. The echoes of this impact maintain to resonate in artwork, literature, and structure, supplying a testament to the enduring strength of classical myths in shaping cultural expression.

Contemporary Literature and Popular Culture

Greek mythology, with its wealthy narratives and timeless subjects, has seamlessly incorporated into modern-day literature and famous way of lifestyles. Its enduring enchantment lies in the profound resonance of its testimonies, iconic characters, and issue topics that consequences traverse generations. From literature to movie, video games, music, or perhaps marketing, Greek mythology maintains to captivate audiences in numerous and compelling techniques.

Film and Television

Epic Tales on the Big and Small Screen: The attraction of Greek mythology extends to the cinematic realm, in which filmmakers reimagine traditional myths for current-day audiences. Blockbusters like "Clash of the Titans" and "Hercules" deliver epic battles and legendary creatures to the huge display screen, providing a seen spectacle rooted in historical memories. Television series which incorporates "Olympus" and "Troy: Fall of a City" retell those myths with contemporary-day storytelling strategies, charming audiences with the undying drama of gods and heroes. Even the Marvel Cinematic Universe includes Greek mythological elements through characters like Thor and Loki, connecting ancient legends with a global purpose market.

Video Games

Interactive Odyssey in Gaming: Greek mythology has determined a colourful home within the global of video video video video games. The "God of War" franchise, as an example, permits gamers to step into the sandals of a vengeful Spartan warrior struggling with in opposition to Greek gods and mythical creatures. "Assassin's Creed Odyssey" transports players to historical Greece, seamlessly mixing myth and ancient fiction in an immersive gaming experience.

Music and Theater

Harmonies and Narratives on Stage: Greek mythology often takes center degree in tune and theater productions. Renowned composers like Richard Strauss and Igor Stravinsky have drawn thought from these historic stories. Strauss's opera "Elektra" delves into the tragic narrative of a vengeful princess, whilst Stravinsky's ballet "Apollo" explores the mythological global with grace and artistic brilliance.

Advertising and Branding

Mythological Symbolism in Marketing: The affect of Greek mythology extends to advertising and branding, in which mythological references evoke a experience of electricity, beauty, and background. Companies leverage the names, symbols, and narratives associated with Greek gods and heroes to installation a connection with their services or products. This strategic use of mythology offers depth and resonance to emblem identities, growing a undying affiliation.

The Lasting Influence of Greek Mythology on Western Civilization

Greek mythology stands as a massive pillar in the intellectual and cultural edifice of Western civilization, weaving its timeless narratives into the very fabric of art, literature, philosophy, language, and societal norms. Here are the profound tactics wherein Greek mythology continues to exert its impact:

Art and Architecture:

Visual Vocabulary: Greek mythology has been a wellspring of concept for artists during facts. Classical sculptures, art work, and mosaics depict gods and heroes, on the same time as mythological motifs grace the friezes and work of artwork of Western structure. The enduring use of Greek architectural elements, which includes columns and pediments, imparts a experience of timelessness and grandeur to homes.

Language and Idioms:

Linguistic Legacy: Greek mythology has bequeathed a linguistic legacy to the English language. Everyday expressions like "Achilles' heel," "Pandora's box," and "Herculean undertaking" hint their origins to the ones ancient testimonies. The term "narcissism" exhibits its roots in the fable of Narcissus, illustrating how mythological narratives have end up embedded in commonplace idioms.

Philosophy and Ethics:

Philosophical Foundations: Greek philosophers, on the side of Plato and Aristotle, covered mythological thoughts into their philosophical frameworks. The moral dilemmas and ethical quandaries explored in Greek myths have turn out to be enduring topics of philosophical inquiry, shaping discussions on justice, morality, and the complexities of the human circumstance.

Science and Astronomy:

Celestial Narratives: Greek mythology has left an indelible mark on the night time time sky. Constellations and celestial objects go through names drawn from mythological characters and stories. The Pleiades, representing the Seven Sisters from the parable of Atlas and Pleione, exemplify how ancient narratives preserve to guide astronomers in figuring out stars and celestial our our bodies.

Political and Societal Influences:

Democratic Ideals: The idea of democracy, originating in historic Greece, shows the beliefs of civic participation and collective preference-making. Greek political and societal systems, as depicted in art and literature, function enduring assets of concept, fostering cultural identity and history interior Western societies.

The enduring impact of Greek mythology on Western civilization transcends time, supplying a profound and undying exploration of the human experience. Its testimonies resonate through the a long time, inviting chronic reinterpretation and mirrored photograph. In adapting, decoding, and reimagining those narratives, human beings, and societies find out a perennial source of idea, intellectual exploration, and a deep connection to the rich tapestry of human subculture.

Chapter 8: Titan Legends

In the difficult tapestry of Greek mythology, the Titans occupy a region this is every foundational and awe-inspiring. These are not mere footnotes within the epics of gods and guys; the Titans have been the primordial entities that shaped the cosmos and laid the muse for the Olympian gods who might take a look at. In this financial ruin titled 'TITAN LEGENDS,' we delve into the charming lives and contributions of those historic beings, starting from the primordial Chaos to Hyperion and Theia, the luminous couple who talented the arena with light and vision.

The Titans were born of Uranus, the sky, and Gaia, the earth—forces so elemental, their very names are synonymous with the domain names they governed. In the ones pages, we are capable of find out the reign of Cronus and Rhea, the transport of the Golden Era, and man or woman reminiscences of Titans like Iapetus and Clymene. These aren't mere myths or testimonies knowledgeable to skip time; the ones are existential philosophies, metaphors for existence and nature, and above all, a searching glass into the values and ideals which have been pivotal in shaping human civilization.

By understanding the Titans, we get a lens into the historic Greek mind, its worry and aspirations, its statistics of justice, circle of relatives, and the herbal worldwide. This economic catastrophe serves as a key to loose up a treasure trove of knowledge that stays as applicable nowadays because it grow to be masses of years inside the past.

The Beginning: Chaos, Uranus, & Gaia

In the begin, there has been Chaos—a boundless, indefinable area, a dark abyss wherein time and bear in mind had no longer but manifested. Picture the big black expanse of a night time time sky with out stars, wherein even the idea of darkness might be an anachronism, for there has been no mild to define it in the course of. Within this swirling cosmic emptiness, the primeval forces of the universe churned and frothed, as although longing for shape and substance.

From this celestial maelstrom emerged Gaia, the Earth Mother. She have come to be each substance and spirit, corporeal yet airy, and it emerge as she who may also provide the stable foundation upon which all of advent may additionally want to stand. A womb of inconceivable modern power, Gaia emanated a profound fertility that could quickly supply upward thrust to all of lifestyles, and all of depend. Just keep in mind the primary peak of a mountain growing from the swirling fog of nothingness—that come to be Gaia, a strong entity growing from the intangible.

Not lengthy after Gaia's formation, Uranus— the Sky Father—materialized to cover her. In assessment to Gaia's grounded, nurturing essence, Uranus become lofty, embodying the vaulted heavens, entire of stars, clouds, and the quintessence of the air. His realm changed into one in every of lofty mind and immeasurable heights, however he positioned his remarkable counterbalance in Gaia's earthly embody. Together, they symbolized the harmony of sky and earth, strong and airy, finite and countless.

Now, the union between Gaia and Uranus grow to be now not in reality symbolic; it changed into an erotic collision of cosmic proportions. From their primordial lovemaking sprang the first beings—the Titans, huge entities endowed with massive power. They may turn out to be the elder gods, the architects of the place's landscapes, and the rulers of elemental forces. But the connection among Gaia and Uranus became extra than a simple romantic tale; it have become a complicated narrative rife with tension.

Uranus, as staggering as he modified into, advanced a despotic nature. Consumed thru his non-public grandeur, he imprisoned some of his Titan offspring deep inside Gaia's womb-like caverns, causing her huge pain. This act sowed the number one seeds of tragedy and discord in the universe. Gaia, a mom scorned and pained, plotted in the direction of him. She long-established a terrific sickle and supplied it to Cronus, absolutely virtually considered one of their Titan sons, who modified into courageous enough to undertaking his father's tyranny. Thus, the extent became set for an epic drama that could eventually culminate within the dethroning of Uranus, and pave the way for the reign of the Titans underneath Cronus.

What is crucial to apprehend right here is that this preliminary narrative symbolizes everlasting subjects: the cycles of beginning, rebellion, and trade. Chaos, Gaia, and Uranus aren't clearly characters in a legendary story, however archetypal forces representing the dynamic interplay amongst nothingness and existence, amongst formless ability and installed reality. This trio of primal entities encapsulates the dialectic of introduction itself—the anxiety, the war, and the everlasting dance among contrasting elements that offers upward thrust to the area as we realise it.

So, as you delve into the legends of Titans, Olympians, and mythical beings that populate the subsequent chapters of this ebook, in no manner forget this genesis story. It's a foundational narrative that paints the cosmic ancient beyond upon which every super tale will unfold. But extra than that, it's a reminder that within the war among chaos and order, ache and advent, predicament and transcendence, we find out the roots not handiest of mythology but of lifestyles itself.

The Reign of Cronus & Rhea

The panorama of power in the Greek pantheon shifted irrevocably whilst Cronus overthrew his father, Uranus. While this act marked a ugly converting of the defend, it additionally ushered in an generation that changed into similarly regal and unsettling. For Cronus, who as quickly as existed in the shadow of his father's celestial glory, ascending the throne alongside his sister-accomplice Rhea meant each dominion and dread.

Cronus and Rhea were now not only a marital alliance; their union represented a balance of power, a concord that stretched from the pointers of Mount Olympus to the depths of the underworld. While Cronus have end up identified for his cunning and ruthless ambition, Rhea brought understanding, grace, and an emotional intensity that her husband lacked. Yet their reign turned into a long way from peaceful. Cronus, haunted with the useful resource of a prophecy that foretold his downfall on the fingers of his offspring, have emerge as consumed by way of the usage of the use of paranoia.

Cronus advanced an insatiable starvation for manage, a yearning so severe that he swallowed his personal youngsters as soon as they were born. The Titan king took perverse comfort in this twisted act, erroneously believing that his preserve on energy became strong with every little one he fed on. Rhea, who cherished her kids deeply and viewed them as extensions of her non-public divinity, became torn apart thru grief. For every beginning, she wept no longer for the difficult paintings's ache however for the inevitable tragedy that would take a look at.

Unable to go through her struggling any similarly, Rhea hatched a plan of subterfuge and salvation. The next time she end up with infant, she gave begin in mystery, entrusting her new infant son, Zeus, to the nymphs of Crete. In his place, she swaddled a stone in little one's garb and furnished it to her unsuspecting husband. Cronus swallowed the stone, none the wiser, cementing his future death and paving the manner for the subsequent wave of divine rulers.

The reign of Cronus and Rhea have grow to be a aggregate of terrific governance and familial disorder. While their dominion over the cosmos delivered forth an technology of relative balance and an evolution of primal powers into greater based totally deitics, it have become tainted through the use of Cronus's all-consuming paranoia. Rhea, embodying the elements of motherhood and understanding, would depart an extended-lasting have an effect on as a deity of resilience, her legacy in the end essential to the rise of the Olympian gods.

For university students delving into historical history or mythology, the reign of Cronus and Rhea serves as a compelling look at inside the complexities of strength and the regularly disastrous outcomes of unchecked ambition. Educators may also moreover need to use this saga as a starting point for discussions on moral values, own family dynamics, and the interaction amongst future and desire. Fans of mythology can understand the gripping narrative, fraught with excessive-stakes emotion and divine politics. Content creators may moreover draw suggestion from this twisted tale of electricity and paranoia, at the same time as vacationers can apprehend the deep cultural context behind many Greek archaeological web sites committed to the ones deities. In essence, the tale of Cronus and Rhea isn't best a story from antiquity; it is a timeless lesson that resonates throughout one-of-a-kind fields and pastimes.

Birth of Era

In the grand tapestry of Greek mythology, the begin of the Golden Era stands as an epoch of monumental importance. After the tumultuous reign of Cronus and Rhea, marked through using betrayal and cyclical violence, the arena yearned for a cutting-edge bankruptcy, a financial disaster of preference and great peace. The age of Titans had its virtues, but it have come to be Zeus—son of Cronus and Rhea—who orchestrated the inception of a great generation that records may fondly consider as 'The Golden Age.'

The rise up led with the useful resource of Zeus in the direction of his father Cronus laid the foundation for the Golden Era. It emerge as a rise up no longer virtually in competition to a tyrannical rule but moreover in opposition to a cycle of familial betrayals that seemed to be the future of the divine. With the defeat of Cronus, Zeus shackled the vintage order and opened a area for novelty, for a cosmos described by way of the usage of regulation and justice, in choice to caprice and oppression. Thus started out the technology of the Olympians, with Zeus at its helm, an era that promised a new manner of governance, no longer only for gods but moreover for mortals.

Zeus hooked up Mount Olympus due to the fact the heavenly capital wherein the Olympians might also need to live. It become more than fine a geographical locale; it changed into a picture of harmony and governance, a much cry from the dark abyss of Tartarus in which Titans were stable away. At Mount Olympus, the gods need to convene, debate, and make alternatives that might govern the arena. It become a fortress of awareness and strength, built upon the collective can also of the cutting-edge pantheon, and it epitomized the zenith of divine civilization.

In this new era, the gods were no longer antagonists however collaborators. Athena, the goddess of statistics, modified into born from Zeus's forehead, genuinely armored, as even though embodying the newfound values of this era—intelligence blended with energy. Apollo introduced song and art work, even as his sister Artemis safeguarded the wild. Demeter observed to the harvests, and Poseidon saved the seas calm. The gods labored in harmony, making sure that the sector flourished. A spirit of benevolence pervaded the land, influencing even the most harsh of hearts.

Under the guideline of Zeus and the Olympians, the relationship amongst gods and mortals grow to be redefined. In the Titan era, gods not regularly interacted with humanity besides for punishment or whim. The Golden Era noticed gods taking walks amongst men, offering steerage or maybe forming relationships. The demigods, heroes like Hercules and Perseus, have become symbols of this new covenant—a hybrid a number of the mortal and the divine, carrying the hopes of both nation-states on their capable shoulders.

The fame quo of justice end up probable the crowning fulfillment of the Golden Era. With Zeus due to the fact the last arbiter, prison hints were established, not just for Olympus however moreover for the Earth. The notion of 'hubris' grow to be born, cautioning every gods and guys towards undue conceitedness. Fate and justice had been now entwined, manifesting the ethical paradigm shift from the chaotic times of the Titans.

Thus, the Golden Era wasn't virtually an age of prosperity but a defining 2nd in cosmic data, even as the antique have grow to be shed for the modern, forging a better international—a worldwide that, for the primary time, held promise for every gods and mortals alike. It marked the zenith of Greek mythology, casting a radiant slight that could shine in the path of records, inspiring generations of university college students, teachers, mythology fans, writers, content material material fabric creators, exercise designers, tourists, and fashionable readers to delve into the rich tapestry of reminiscences and understanding that emanate from this outstanding time.

Tales of Iapetus & Clymene

Within the expansive sphere of Greek mythologies lies the tale of Iapetus and Clymene, one of the lesser-identified however difficult memories imparting Titans of immeasurable importance. Iapetus, often dubbed the "Piercer," have become one of the sons of Uranus and Gaia. His consort Clymene, a daughter of Oceanus and Tethys, gave him four noteworthy children: Atlas, Prometheus, Epimetheus, and Menoetius. The lineage of Iapetus is subsequently complete of beings who would possibly later play huge roles in shaping the mythological global and beyond. However, in advance than delving into the lives in their illustrious offspring, it's pivotal to spotlight Iapetus and Clymene themselves.

Iapetus became a picture of mortality and the human lifespan; his very name may be derived from the word 'iapto,' which means that "to wound" or "pierce," indicating a existence lessen quick or limited via the confines of mortality. On the alternative hand, Clymene have come to be a personification of reputation and infamy, a dichotomy that performs out conspicuously within the lives of their children. Their union represents a excellent fusion amongst mortality and renown, barriers and aspirations.

Iapetus turned into often appeared as an embodiment of the West, a geographical term but additionally an ideological concept, representing the unknown, the unexplored, and, to a point, the inevitable decline—the sunset of existence. His being become for this reason imbued with a feel of poetic forlornness. In evaluation, Clymene's reputation for fame and infamy offers her an almost liminal first-class, oscillating amongst adoration and detestation. The interaction among those standards is a exceptional spectacle of cosmic contradictions, exhibited through their progeny who, for higher or worse, exemplified the attributes of their mother and father.

For instance, Atlas have become stressed with keeping up the sky—a task of ceaseless toil, a mortal's plight taken to divine extremity. Prometheus, the fireside-bringer, resonated with Clymene's duality by using using being a hero and a crook simultaneously. He stole fireside to gain humanity but modified into with out end punished for his audacious act. Epimetheus, who grow to be taken into consideration unwise for accepting Pandora and her notorious subject, embodied human frailty, an extension of Iapetus's embodiment of mortality. Menoetius, but, changed into a god of violent anger and rash moves, symbolizing how the dual natures of his dad and mom also can spiral into outright destructiveness.

The love story amongst Iapetus and Clymene isn't one complete of grand gestures or heroic deeds, but it's far profoundly telling of the values and dichotomies that would take region in their descendants. While their union may not be celebrated with the equal fervor as other divine pairings, the ramifications in their assembly could echo via records, for their offspring carried the burden of the world, pretty actually, and figuratively long-established the human scenario. Therefore, to apprehend the Tales of Iapetus and Clymene is to delve deep into the philosophical underpinnings of Greek mythology, spotting that even lesser-recognized figures have a element in weaving the tough tapestry that has captivated humanity for hundreds of years.

So, whether you're a pupil unraveling the complex threads of historical myths, a instructor searching for compelling narratives to supplement your class, or simply an enthusiast entranced through the lore of gods and titans, the story of Iapetus and Clymene offers a wealthy, nuanced lens thru which to view the entangled geographical regions of mortality and legacy. The paradoxes in their tale may additionally need to function idea-horrifying material for writers and content material creators, on the same time as their shiny characters provide fertile ground for exercise designers. And, for individuals who plan to tread upon Greek soil or scale the heights of Mount Olympus, knowledge this story can also furthermore furnish a layer of profundity in your adventure.

Chapter 9: The Olympian Beginnings

As the echoes of the Titanomachy quieted and the vintage order gave way to the trendy, a very particular air of expectancy crammed the cosmos. This is the breathtaking chapter of the Olympians, gods who have been markedly distinct from their Titan forebears in their information of electricity, justice, and human affairs. Gone have been the instances whilst Cronus and Rhea dictated the pace and nature of the divine reign. Now, a more youthful generation, headed via Zeus and flanked thru his myriad siblings and youngsters, prepared to rewrite the edicts of introduction. This bankruptcy will navigate thru their beginnings—the framework they installation, their inner dynamics, the physical and metaphysical regions they occupied, and the cosmological aesthetics they preferred. No longer were the gods a ways flung and precis entities; they have come to be closer to human understanding, full of relatable goals, feelings, and flaws. Understanding this era is critical not definitely to understand the reign of Olympians, however additionally to make revel in of the cultural, mythological, or even moral implications in their reign for the human race.

The Rule of Cronus & Rhea

The reign of Cronus and Rhea occupies a pivotal function in the grand narrative of Greek mythology, marking the twilight of Titan rule and the sunrise of the Olympian age. However, their governance wasn't best a fleeting interlude; it modified right into a complicated and nuanced period, imbued with each glory and infamy, virtues and vices. Cronus, who had overthrown his father Uranus to emerge as the king of the Titans, end up every a smart and ruthless chief. His rule embodied the paradoxes of manage, wielding authority with a calculating thoughts that is probably each beneficent and tyrannical.

Rhea, his sister and queen, became his counterbalance. While Cronus ruled with an iron fist, Rhea provided the emotional and ethical compass desired for their rule. She come to be the motherly discern, not definitely to their kids—the Olympian gods like Zeus, Hestia, Hera, Hades, Poseidon, and Demeter—but additionally to the arena that they ruled. Her nurturing spirit added a semblance of compassion into an technology in any other case defined through Cronus' iron-willed rule.

If Cronus changed into the embodiment of the sky and celestial order, Rhea become the essence of Earth, existence-giving and nurturing. This celestial partnership represented a synthesis of opposites, the sky and the earth conjoined in a divine marriage, casting a version for the hierarchical cosmos. But the relationship had its fissures, considerably Cronus' paranoia approximately being overthrown by using his kids, a prophecy that strong a darkish shadow over their reign.

Driven via the priority of dropping strength, Cronus swallowed his new toddler youngsters whole. This act stands as a chilling testomony to the consequences of unrestrained authority and the anxieties that include it. Here, we see the underbelly of governance and the ethical compromises often made to keep energy. Rhea, horrified by means of the shortage of her kids and angered thru the usage of Cronus' betrayal, orchestrated an hard scheme to shop her youngest, Zeus, replacing him with a stone wrapped in swaddling garments. Cronus swallowed the stone, assuming he had over again thwarted destiny.

The act of Rhea saving Zeus symbolizes the resilience and ingenuity frequently displayed within the face of dire times. It's a stark reminder that even inside the darkest of times, there may be a glimmer of need, regularly represented through clever stratagems and the indomitable spirit of a mom. This act laid the foundation for the eventual defeat of Cronus and the upward push of the Olympian gods, underlining the importance of Rhea's position in shaping the destiny.

Their rule ended at the equal time as Zeus, nurtured in mystery, grew up to challenge his father. The foxy intelligence and brute power of Zeus might be considered a harmonious mixture of both Cronus' authoritarian records and Rhea's nurturing affect. Ultimately, the rule of thumb of thumb of Cronus and Rhea is a microcosm of fantastic standards—order and chaos, authority and compassion, information and folly. It serves as a cautionary story about the perils and virtues of management, and the ethical complexities inherent in governance.

The Battle of Titans: Titanomachy

The sky hung heavy with anticipation due to the fact the first mild of sunrise cracked over the horizon. The gods and goddesses, new baby Olympians, drew up their plans in mystery councils. Here they huddled, a long way eliminated from the thrones and palaces of their Titan mother and father, the architects of the universe. In this celestial drama, Zeus, the youngest son of Cronus and

Rhea, assumed the mantle of leadership. But what control it become to oppose your very non-public lineage, to stand towards folks that gave the cosmos its shape and substance. Yet, Zeus and his siblings had no special desire, for his or her very existence have become threatened underneath the reign of the Titans, in particular their father, Cronus.

This come to be a civil conflict, now not genuinely of familial ties but of cosmic significance. On one detail were the Titans—historic, powerful, almost summary in their cosmic roles. Cronus held sway over time; Hyperion, over the sun; and Oceanus, over the boundless sea. On the alternative issue have been the Olympians, more energizing in their divinity but untested of their electricity—Zeus alongside with his lightning bolt, Poseidon along alongside together with his trident, and Hades collectively collectively with his dark helm that rendered him invisible. They have been united below a commonplace reason: freedom from the oppressive rule of their forebears.

It is stated that the war raged for ten grueling years. Each aspect had its allies and champions. The Titans had the fearsome one-hundred-passed Hecatoncheires and the tremendous Typhon, whose very gaze ought to turn a mortal into stone. The Olympians sought help from the Cyclopes, professional smiths who cast Zeus's lightning bolt, Poseidon's trident, and Hades's Helm of Darkness. The stakes could not be higher. The battlefield grow to be the very universe itself, a labyrinthine expanse wherein rivers flowed backward and stars blinked out of life fine to re-light some region else.

Every skirmish had its expenses, each victory its sacrifices. Prometheus, the Titan who sided with the Olympians, used his foresight to count on the Titans' actions. But even he couldn't foresee each final effects. In the pivotal battle, Zeus unleashed a storm so ferocious that even the Titans needed to shield their eyes. With that distraction, he hurled his lightning bolt, solid in celestial fireside, at his father Cronus, crippling him.

Seizing the on the spot, the Olympians rallied and drove the Titans decrease again, pushing them into the dark abyss of Tartarus.

The warfare emerge as acquired, but at super charge. The universe might undergo the scars forever—a broken throne, a severed familial tie, the echoes of thunder regardless of the fact that resounding inside the sky. But with the Titans' downfall, a modern day order rose. Zeus claimed his father's throne and divided the dominion of the arena among his siblings. Yet, the reminiscence of Titanomachy remained a ghost that could hold-out them, a cautionary tale whispered inside the corridors of Mount Olympus.

This tremendous war wasn't handiest a violent schism; it grow to be a converting of the shield, a change of cosmic governance. It hooked up the Olympian deities as the brand new rulers, allowing them the liberty to infuse the area with more nuanced virtues and vices, subtleties and complexities. The Titans, confined to Tartarus, have emerge as symbolic of an historical order, one that had to break to make way for the cutting-edge.

So the gods may also need to mention, as they seemed again at the chaos and the bloodshed: it needed to appear. For from the ruins of Titanomachy, a latest era dawned. It is probably an era characterized not virtually by the usage of divine rule however by using way of human memories, mythic tales, and cultural narratives that preserve to shape us to in the mean time. And this is why the Battle of the Titans, the Titanomachy, holds this kind of pivotal vicinity inside the records of the gods and of the region. It end up the crucible wherein a brand new age have become cast—a turbulent but crucial passage that defined what need to come after.

Thus, Titanomachy serves as an everlasting testomony to the struggles for freedom, for justice, and for a higher international— struggles that, in a unmarried form or a few unique, hold to reverberate via the corridors of time.

Partitioning the World

In the aftermath of the chaotic Titanomachy, the newly risen Olympian gods observed themselves on pinnacle of things of a global that have been each torn asunder and laid bare. The reign of the Titans had ended, and the divine generational shift echoed thru the cosmos like a thunderclap, sending tremors thru the lands, the oceans, and the celestial spheres. Yet, the world became though a canvas—undefined, formless, and looking ahead to the brushstrokes that could offer it form and order. And so, inside the council halls of Mount Olympus, draped in clouds and hidden from mortal eyes, the gods convened to partition the world that that they had actually obtained.

The environment became thick with every possibility and anxiety, similar to that of a typhoon quietly gathering strain. Zeus, who had led his siblings and allies to victory, took the mantle of manage all all over again, but cautiously so. His gaze surveyed his council, from Athena's understanding-crammed eyes to Apollo's radiant face, from Demeter's nurturing presence to Poseidon's sea-like, impenetrable eyes. "We have freed the area from the clutches of tyranny," he commenced out, "but a rulerless global is but a supply without a helmsman; it is upon us to guide it."

It modified into Poseidon who spoke first. "The sea is my dominion," he declared, his voice as deep as ocean trenches. "It is a international of its very personal, chaotic and serene, fierce and forgiving. I lay claim to it, to be its keeper and determine."

His phrases washed over the gathering like a tide. The other gods nodded; it have become a turning into dominion for one so tempestuous and deep. Demeter spoke next. "Then permit the land be mine," she stated softly. "Its fields and forests, its mountains and valleys. I shall breathe existence into the earth, permit flora bloom and harvests ripen."

Hera, the Queen beside Zeus, interjected at the side of her claim to the hearth and circle of relatives. Athena determined on expertise and strategic warfare; Apollo the sun, tune, and humanities; his dual sister, Artemis, the moon and the barren location; Hermes will be the messenger, bridging the worlds; Aphrodite claimed love; and Ares, battle. Each took a issue of lifestyles, carving out their very private realm of have an impact on.

But this have become no longer pretty a whole lot dominion; it changed into about identification, approximately the type of gods they may come to be and the legacy they would leave. Each knew that with their options, they were moreover deciding on the values that they may champion, the virtues and the vices they may encompass.

In a single, cosmic breath, the arena became divided and but unified. A new order end up etched into the fabric of truth. Mortals might now pray to Poseidon for regular passage within the path of the seas, to Demeter for bountiful harvests, to Hera for familial peace, and so forth. The gods have become architects of the world's phenomena and clients of its myriad components.

This partitioning have become a cosmic blueprint, an unstated agreement amongst gods and humans, nature and nurture. It become a declaration that even in a global teeming with caprice and unpredictability, there has been a semblance of order, a tapestry woven from many threads, each ruled thru using a hand of divinity. In partitioning the world, the Olympian gods did no longer truly carve up territories; they laid the cornerstones of a complex, intertwined existence, a colourful worldwide of divine-human interactions, in which each prayer had an ear, each motion a result, and each life a cause.

Gods' Throne

High atop Mount Olympus, properly above the cloud line wherein mortal eyes couldn't determine the majesty, stood the throne room of the gods. Not genuinely an assemblage of chairs or ornate furnishings, this turn out to be an area consecrated thru divine will and cosmic order. Here, celestial shape spread out itself in structures not viable by using manner of the usage of human artisanship. The partitions, if one must name them that, had been interwoven beams of slight and shadow, solidified whispers of time and space held in a lattice of sacred geometry.

In the middle of it all was the throne of Zeus, ordinary from an amalgamation of heavenly substances that had no earthly analog. Thunderstorms had been woven into its material, and lightning flashed internal its depths, taking pictures the essence of Zeus's dominion over the sky and climate. Seated right here, the King of Gods issued judgments that resonated via the mortal and immortal worlds, shaping future and upholding cosmic balance.

Flanking Zeus were unique thrones, each remarkable but complementary, embodying the essence of the deity it have become crafted for. Hera's throne changed into an difficult production of ivory and peacock feathers, taking pics her stylish beauty and eager, watchful eyes. Poseidon's was a tempest in a chair, swirling tides and roaring waves personified inside its form. Athena's, carved from olive wood and engraved with sigils of information, appeared to contemplate its environment with an unseen gaze.

Yet, the thrones were now not mere seats. They had been conduits of power, focal elements via which the gods channeled their will into the Universe. Their alignment changed into essential for the touchy balance between chaos and order, for the tapestry of life and loss of existence, love and strife, to be maintained. Through those thrones, the gods must have a have a look at each nook of life, from the depths of Tartarus to the edges of the mortal realm.

What might also seem paradoxical was that those divine thrones additionally acted as restraints, obstacles upon their occupants. The gods had been certain to their roles, to the spheres of impact each throne represented. While Zeus need to summon storms and control the skies, he couldn't step into Poseidon's aquatic location without inflicting a cosmic imbalance that even he couldn't rectify.

As conduits, the thrones have been additionally bridges. They related the gods not simplest to their domain names however to every exclusive, fostering a complicated network of alliances, responsibilities, and, sure, even feuds. Here, they will consult, argue, and scheme, attaining options that would ripple through existence. The harmony or discord amongst them manifested in natural phenomena, affecting mortal lives in ways that human beings need to slightly start to recognize.

The room was without time; it have become everlasting. Days and nights cycled interior seconds, and but a second must stretch on for eons. Here, on this seat of divine governance, every communicate had gravity, each selection become full-size, and every judgment set in movement a sequence of sports activities that might direction thru the veins of the Universe itself.

In essence, the throne room have grow to be no longer simply an area. It changed into a residing, respiratory entity—a collective popularity of divine reason and cosmic order. A coronary coronary heart, perhaps, beating in rhythm with the grander cosmos, pumping the lifeblood of destiny via the arteries of truth. And at its center have become the unspoken acknowledgment amongst all gods that regardless of their squabbles and conflicts, their thrones have been hewn from the same celestial material, linking them in an inextricable community of cosmic governance that had common, and could preserve to form, the destiny of all things.

Chapter 10: Trinity Of Power

In the celestial tapestry that is Greek mythology, some threads shimmer extra vividly than the others. These are the threads that entwine to shape the Trinity of Power—Zeus, Hera, and Poseidon. While in advance chapters guided us via the dawn of the Titans and the rise up that brought about Olympian rule, this bankruptcy objectives to delve deeper into the essence of the deities who wield the most sturdy impact over the cosmos and human lives alike. Zeus, the almighty King of the Gods; Hera, his in addition ambitious Queen; and Poseidon, the Lord of the Seas, are not simply characters in ancient memories but the embodiment of traditional forces that have inspired manner of lifestyles, religion, and man or woman ideals for millennia. Students, teachers, mythology fanatics, and creators alike will discover the narratives in this economic catastrophe valuable, each tale imbued with statistics which have been surpassed down generations however often remain untold in preferred textbooks. As we journey thru their historic recollections, we will discover the complexities that make the ones gods relatable but awe-inspiring, terrifying but comforting. This financial ruin endeavors to shed light on these paragons of energy, every wielding their scepters of have an impact on over domain names each tangible and summary.

King of Gods: Zeus

Stepping into the location of mythology, one can not forget the indelible impact of Zeus, the King of Gods. The ruler of Mount Olympus become someone with an arsenal of paradoxes—awesome however wrong, decisive yet capricious. His name by myself consists of a legacy interwoven with thunderbolts, divine interventions, and convoluted relationships both divine and mortal. The recollections of Zeus take us down labyrinthine corridors of philosophy and ritual, into the human psyche and a ways above it. They are the memories that have sculpted and personified strength and control for eons, serving as allegories and commands as lots as they feature reminiscences.

The beginning of Zeus is itself a riveting story, teeming with the intrigue of revolt closer to his father Cronus, the preceding King of the Titans. He changed into hidden away within the dim recesses of the island of Crete, a protracted manner from the prying eyes of a father who had swallowed his siblings, to develop and cross returned for retribution. This narrative of a usurper god unseating the preceding ruler have end up an archetypal myth, reverberating for the duration of more than one cultures and theological constructs. It set the extent for Zeus' overarching role as an icon of overthrowing oppressive authority—a modern clothed in divine raiment.

As if acknowledging his current origins, Zeus delivered a specific type of governance to the divine realm. He presided over the Council of Gods like a politician who understood the power of worldwide members of the own family and compromise. No longer changed into the rule of thumb of the gods a despotic one. It modified proper right into a complicated, if now not virtually democratic, body wherein more than one voices had been heard, if no longer constantly heeded. This technique to divine governance extended Zeus past simply the most powerful of the gods to a ruler who exhibited statesmanship, albeit divine in nature.

And then there are stories of Zeus' love affairs—each a tale unto itself, a complicated interaction of lust, trickery, and outcomes. Stories like that of his union with Leda, a liaison that brought approximately the start of the superb Helen, have end up emblematic of Zeus' everlasting impact on mortal lives and histories. Through those testimonies, Zeus morphed proper right into a god who changed into now not clearly a king inside the heavens however moreover a remarkable player in human affairs. His complex relationships illustrated the blurred lines most of the divine and the human, frequently serving as classes for mortal conduct.

Yet, for all his grandeur and complexity, Zeus changed into in no manner past scrutiny. He emerge as now not an immaculate entity however a deity with weaknesses and proclivities that reflected human foibles. His wrath become fierce, exemplified via the story of Prometheus, whose punishment for stealing fireplace become a excessive instance of Zeus' inflexible justice. And on the same time as the ones recollections have been retold limitless instances, their complexities no matter the reality that lend themselves to new interpretations, from vital examinations in academia to progressive retellings in popular culture.

The memories of Zeus stay a cornerstone of Western mythology and idea, a chain of layered narratives that provide glimpses into the human condition whilst they find out the complexities of divine electricity. By facts those historic recollections, we unravel now not without a doubt the fabric of a mythical past however additionally the complex weave of humanity's ongoing dating with authority, justice, and morality.

Queen Hera: Ancient Tales

If there can be one deity within the Greek pantheon whose very essence pulsates with intrigue and energy, it is Hera. Often reduced to being in fact the accomplice of Zeus, she is a lot greater—Queen of the Gods, matron of family and marriage, and a image of relentless will and divine poise. Hera's ancient memories do now not actually serve as adjuncts to the memories of her husband or her turbulent marriage. They exist as stand-on my own sagas of a goddess who knew the fine details of authority, and who must maneuver thru cosmic politics with a finesse that would extraordinary be divine.

As a younger goddess, Hera become no stranger to the underhanded politics of Mount Olympus. One specific tale devices the tone for her cleverness. The gods' nectar, their deliver of immortality, come to be carefully guarded. Yet Hera, the use of her wits and attraction, efficiently deceived the guards and made away with a vial. She wasn't stuck, but absolutely everyone knew best someone as savvy as Hera have to pull off the sort of heist. This wasn't an act of insurrection but a statement of her latent powers. She confirmed early on that she had the choice and the intelligence to reap some thing she deemed vital.

Hera's marriage to Zeus is one of the most talked-about unions in mythology. What many don't apprehend is the subversion of expectancies Hera delivered thru it. The rite itself come to be celestial, graced through every divine entity and seasoned with cosmic melodies. The sacred bond did now not tie Hera down, but increased her have an impact on. While Zeus roamed, Hera ruled, and her reign became no longer a silent one. She issued decrees, mediated divine quarrels, and finished judgments that even Zeus could now not dare overturn. She changed into the stableness to his excesses and the gravity to his flights of celestial fancy.

One of Hera's most well-known interactions is with Hercules, the son of Zeus and Alcmena, a mortal. Despite famous opinion, Hera's trials for Hercules have been not petty moves of a spurned spouse however calculated alternatives of a deity who has a realm to protect. Hera understood the cosmic stability, and Hercules' feats threatened it. Her trials have been now not tests of his strength by myself however additionally of his man or woman. Could he be a demi-god who upheld the standards that the gods, mainly Hera, held pricey? The twelve labors of Hercules can be his story, however it is Hera's requirements that he had to meet.

Beyond the politics and power plays, Hera modified into additionally a deity deeply rooted in the sanctity of marriage and own family. She blessed unions and cursed infidelities, a two-sided coin of the identical divine best she represented. Couples prayed to her for longevity and constancy, and he or she or he or he heard. Her ancient tales show that her wrath end up fearsome, but so have become her love and need. She ought to make barren lands fertile and cradle a crying toddler to sleep with an insignificant idea.

By delving into those historical stories of Hera, we discover a goddess who's every complex and compelling, who cannot be boxed into stereotypes or simplistic narratives. Hera, Queen of the Gods, worrying conditions us to appearance beyond the superficial and respect the multifaceted, the nuanced, and the profoundly influential roles she performs within the annals of Greek mythology.

Lord of Seas: Poseidon

In the outstanding halls of Mount Olympus, wherein the whims and wills of gods shifted like gusts of wind, Poseidon, Lord of Seas, harbored a internet site a protracted manner less capricious however as strong as any of his celestial circle of relatives. Much has been said of Zeus, the sky-living king, and Hera, the queen; but, no story of Olympian may can forgo the ruler whose trident stirred oceans, gave shape to islands, and soothed similarly to terrified the mariners of historic days. Poseidon's story is not without a doubt a footnote in the annals of divine electricity— it's miles a saga of creation, of struggle, and ultimately, a testament to the unsung intricacies of an professional that reigns now not within the heavens, however within the deep abyss.

A primordial deity, Poseidon emerged into cosmic focus alongside Zeus and Hades, his brothers, whilst the age of Titans gave manner to that of Olympians. While Zeus claimed the skies and Hades the Underworld, Poseidon determined his dominion in the waters—rivers, lakes, and generally, the expansive seas that linked every civilization. Yet his electricity have become now not confined in reality to realms aquatic. The Earthshaker, as he end up often called, held sway over earthquakes, his anger or mere restlessness reverberating through the planet's crust. It come to be stated that Poseidon should form landscapes with a trifling flick of his wrist, birthing new islands as gadgets or likely as tokens of divine whimsy.

But permit us to no longer forget Poseidon the Lawgiver, an detail often overshadowed via his tempestuous recognition. The prison pointers of the ocean have been Poseidon's scriptures, and each sailor, fisherman, and explorer have grow to be his disciple, knowingly or otherwise. Those who defied the marine codes, or dared to devote sacrilege in his waters, may meet his wrath within the form of sea monsters like Scylla and Charybdis, or natural catastrophes that left no room for doubt approximately the sea's unforgiving draw close. Yet, for folks who paid homage, Poseidon may be a merciful god, calming the seas for secure passage and filling nets with ok seize. Such grow to be the duality of the Lord of Seas—a benevolent issuer and an unforgiving adjudicator.

Lovers of lore often keep in mind Poseidon's trysts and rivalries. His romantic escapades brought about a myriad of offspring—heroes, monsters, and divine entities that straddle the road amongst both. One ought to factor out Theseus, begotten from an affair with a mortal lady, Aethra, who could later slay the Minotaur; or the winged horse Pegasus, born from his affair with Medusa. However, Poseidon become now not a god to undergo offense gently. His opposition with Athena for the patronage of Athens observed him conjuring a saltwater spring from the Acropolis, a display of power that, despite the fact that trumped by means of manner of using Athena's olive tree, symbolized his ever-sturdy effect and attain.

Beyond the tapestry of myths and worship, Poseidon's effect resonates on more than one layers. From the existential know-how of the ocean as an ever-changing yet normal pressure, to the cultural symbolism of naval would possibly likely or exploration, the maritime deity has left an indelible mark. For students of historical statistics and fantasy, Poseidon's story serves as a complicated knowledge of the manner early societies conceptualized natural phenomena, justice, and divine caprice. For instructors and mythology fans, it gives a rich textual content of ancient ethics, human endeavors, and the manifestation of powers that, at the same time as not worshipped in temples, however keep humanity in awe.

In the cease, Poseidon, Lord of Seas, isn't truely a figure to be reckoned with but an extended lasting image of our innate and complex relationship with the sector's oceans. His stories are each an historical mirrored picture and a contemporary lesson—on concord, on admire, and on the awe-inspiring, often unfathomable forces that govern our world. Such is the legacy of Poseidon: now not best a god of the seas, however a deity whose complexities make him an eternal a part of human way of life and knowledge.

With this, the tale of Poseidon in our Trinity of Power stands now not as a very particular epic but as a story that flows similar to the waters he regulations, and not using a lead to sight shaping and reshaping the contours of human belief and civilization.

As we near the financial wreck in this powerful trio of divine forces, it is important to understand how their memories have woven themselves into the very fabric of our collective interest. Zeus, Hera, and Poseidon are not genuinely historical gods limited to the climate-worn stones of Grecian temples; they are living entities that form our belief of strength, justice, and nature. Students will find out the richness of those testimonies to be an critical addition to their educational hobbies. Teachers will discover new avenues to invigorate have a look at room dialogue, the use of those memories as a framework for exploring ethical dilemmas and societal values. Lovers of mythology and creators can experience the endless concept furnished by means of the usage of the use of the ones

164

recollections, full of heroism, betrayal, love, and wrath. As for pastime designers, the attributes and conflicts that surround the ones gods serve as an extremely good template for crafting immersive worlds. Tourists can walk the lands of Greece with a heightened sense of the testimonies that imbue its very soil, and favored readers are provided a passport to a realm of splendor and intrigue. This bankruptcy, it's miles was hoping, has enriched your understanding of a international in which gods walk amongst us, invisible but all-encompassing. May your creativeness sail upon Poseidon's seas, take to the air on the whispers of Zeus, and locate home in the protective gaze of Hera.

Chapter 11: Zeus The King Of The Gods

In this monetary break, we will enter the kingdom of Zeus, the effective quality god of Olympus, who guidelines the heavens and exerts have an impact on overall gods and mortals. Get equipped to find out the majestic determine this is Zeus and the recollections that surround him.

The Rise of Zeus

Zeus modified into born from Cronos and Rhea , titan gods who ruled the universe until then. However, Kronos feared that his children would possibly dethrone him, so he swallowed them as speedy as they have been born. Zeus escaped this cruel fate and grew up in thriller. When the time got here, he led a rebellion towards Kronos, releasing his brothers and sisters and becoming the new ruler of the gods.

The Dominion of Zeus

As king of the gods, Zeus ruled the heavens, controlling lightning and thunder with lightning as his photo. He come to be furthermore the guardian of criminal pointers and divine justice, intervening in conflicts and judging gods and mortals.

Relationships and descendants

Zeus changed into seemed for his many amorous adventures, which led to a chain of demigod and goddess youngsters. One of his most famous unions modified into collectively along with his sister Hera, who've come to be his associate and queen of the gods. However, Zeus additionally had affairs with severa different deities and mortals.

The Myths of Zeus

Among the outstanding-recognized myths concerning Zeus is the conflict in opposition to the Titans, the liberation of Prometheus, the arrival of the human race and the well-known episode of tying Prometheus to a rock for stealing fire from the gods.

The Symbolism of Zeus

Zeus represented not simplest celestial power, however also justice and authority. His figure come to be worshiped inside the direction of Ancient Greece, and masses of temples have been erected in his honor.

Hera The Queen of the Gods

In this bankruptcy, we're able to delve into the complexities of the goddess Hera, the wife of Zeus and the queen of the Greek gods. We will find out his particular character, his myths and his essential function in Greek mythology.

The Origin of Hera

Hera was born to the titans Cronus and Rhea , making her the sister and wife of Zeus. She was reputable because the goddess of marriage, circle of relatives and motherhood, but her story is complete of worrying conditions and conflicts.

Hera's Personality

Hera became regarded for her jealous and vengeful nature. She changed into frequently angered with the useful useful resource of Zeus's infidelities and lashed out punishments in opposition to his mistresses and illegitimate youngsters. However, she have become additionally a protecting goddess of married girls and the corporation of marriage.

The Myths of Hera

Among the most famous myths related to Hera is the episode wherein she tried to usurp Zeus's throne and her competition with Heracles (Hercules), Zeus' son with a mortal girl. She set him impossible disturbing situations as a part of her revenge, however Heracles triumphed over they all.

Temples and Worship

Hera was worshiped in some unspecified time in the destiny of Ancient Greece, and lots of temples had been constructed in her honor. The Temple of Hera at Olympia modified into in particular well-known and hosted the Olympic Games in her honor.

Hera's Role in the Greek Pantheon

Hera performed a pivotal characteristic in Greek mythology as the partner of Zeus and queen of the gods. His conflicts and rivalries with other gods added intensity to the mythological narrative.

Poseidon - Lord of the Seas

In this economic disaster, we're able to enter the kingdom of Poseidon, the god of the seas and oceans in Greek mythology. Get prepared to discover the effective lord of the waters and find out the charming testimonies that surround him.

The Origin of Poseidon

Poseidon come to be the son of the titans Cronus and Rhea , making him the brother of Zeus and Hades. He dominated the big oceans and had the trident as his unique photograph, a weapon that gave him control over the waters.

Dominion over the Seas

Poseidon exercised superb dominion over the waters, controlling the seas, rivers and all marine beings. Greek sailors frequently called upon him for safety in the route in their trips at sea.

The Rivalry with Athena

One of the most famous reminiscences concerning Poseidon is his dispute with Athena for the patronage of Athens, an essential Greek city-usa. They competed to present a present to the town, and Poseidon struck with a trident that created a spring of salt water, while Athena supplied the town with an olive tree. Athena obtained the competition, and Athens have turn out to be well-known for its olive timber.

Poseidon and the Myths

Poseidon has been concerned in numerous mythological tales, collectively together along with his function in the delusion of the hero Theseus and the myth of Medusa. Its have an impact on over the ocean additionally extended to earthquakes, as it changed into taken into consideration answerable for seismic shocks.

Worship and Cult

Due to his importance to sailors and the relevance of the seas to Ancient Greece, Poseidon modified into widely worshiped in the route of Greek territory. Many temples were committed to him, along with the Temple of Poseidon at Sounion , which supplied a lovely view of the Aegean Sea.

Chapter 12: Athena The Goddess Of Wisdom

In this bankruptcy, we're capable of delve into the arena of Athena, the goddess of statistics, approach and craftsmanship in Greek mythology. Get prepared to satisfy the goddess who personifies intellect and intelligence.

The Origin of Athena

Athena is one of the most high-quality goddesses on Olympus and is understood for her exquisite information. She modified into born in a completely unique way, proper now from the pinnacle of her father, Zeus, after he swallowed her mom Metis, the goddess of prudence, out of fear that she may want to deliver beginning to a son extra powerful than him. Athena's transport symbolizes the search for information and intelligence.

Athena's Personality

Athena grow to be visible as a serene, strategic and prudent goddess. Unlike many extraordinary deities, she modified into no longer associated with out of manage passions. Instead, she became stated for her not unusual sense, discernment, and capability to treatment conflicts.

War and Strategy

Although Athena come to be a goddess of know-how, she furthermore had abilties in method and war. She changed into regularly depicted with a spear and shield, representing her position as protector of Athens and her ability to skillfully behavior battles.

Athens: The City Dedicated to Athena

The town of Athens end up named after Athena, and she turn out to be the city's consumer goddess. Athens changed into regarded for its reputation on schooling, philosophy, and the arts, reflecting the values of the goddess of data.

Mythology and Legends of Athena

Athena turn out to be involved in several extremely good Greek myths, collectively along with her competition with Poseidon for possession of Athens, her beneficial resource to the hero Perseus in stopping Medusa, and her function as mentor to heroes consisting of Odysseus.

Apollo The God of Arts and Music

In this financial break, we are able to delve into the sector of Apollo, the god of arts, tune, and sunlight hours in Greek mythology. Get prepared to satisfy the deity who personifies harmony and beauty.

The Origin of Apollo

Apollo have become one of the children of Zeus and Leto, and he and his twin sister, Artemis, had been born on the island of Delos . Apollo grow to be regarded for his beauty and fashion, and modified into regularly portrayed as an impeccable extra youthful man.

Apollo and Music

Apollo have become a professional musician, playing the lyre masterfully. He became additionally the leader of the Muses, the goddesses of artwork and creativity, and end up respected because of the reality the god of song, poetry, and prophecy.

The God of Sunlight

Apollo became furthermore related to the solar and light, illuminating the location with his sun chariot. This connection with the solar represented his have an impact on as a god of clarity and highbrow illumination.

The Oracle of Delphi

One of the maximum famous factors of Apollo have become the oracle at Delphi, in which priestesses known as Pythonesses conveyed divine prophecies. The oracle's solutions have been considerably legitimate and well-known with the resource of Greeks and foreigners.

Apollo and Daphne

One of the satisfactory-seemed myths approximately Apollo is that of his pursuit of the nymph Daphne, who became transformed right into a tree to escape his attacks. This shows his duality as god of beauty and perdition.

Artemis - The Goddess of Hunting and Nature

In this chapter, we will enter the kingdom of Artemis, the goddess of looking, wild nature and the moon in Greek mythology. Get geared up to meet the goddess who personifies untouched nature and backbone.

The Origin of Artemis

Artemis have end up the daughter of Zeus and Leto, and twin sister of Apollo. She come to be born first and helped her mom during Apollo's start, demonstrating her protecting and compassionate nature.

The Ultimate Huntress

Artemis turn out to be called the goddess of hunting and vegetation and fauna. She changed into frequently depicted with a bow and arrows, and her searching abilties have been mythical. She covered animals and forests, making sure the stability of nature.

The Protector of Women and Children

In addition to her feature as goddess of looking, Artemis changed into additionally seen due to the reality the protector of girls and children. She changed into in particular honored thru pregnant and laboring girls.

The Moon and Nature

Artemis grow to be also associated with the moon and changed into often represented as a lunar goddess. His reference to the moon pondered his dominance over the night time and his have an impact on on nature.

Chapter 13: Aphrodite The Goddess Of Love And Beauty

In this bankruptcy, we're capable of discover the charming global of Aphrodite, the goddess of affection, splendor and ardour in Greek mythology. Get prepared to meet the deity who embodies the strength of love and enchantment.

The Origin of Aphrodite

Aphrodite is one of the most well-known goddesses in Greek mythology and has a unique beginning. According to legend, she turn out to be born from the waves of the sea after Kronos lessen off Uranus' genitals and threw them into the sea. She emerged from the waters on a sea shell, an iconic photo that represents her.

The Goddess of Love and Beauty

Aphrodite grow to be the goddess of love, ardour and beauty. She turn out to be often portrayed as a cute, seductive girl whose beauty mesmerized gods and mortals alike.

Relationships and Marriages

Aphrodite changed into married to Hephaestus, the god of blacksmiths; however had severa fans, collectively with Ares, the god of struggle, and Adonis, a handsome more youthful mortal. Their romances often sparked jealousy and warfare among the gods.

Aphrodite and Eternal Love

Aphrodite changed into answerable for promoting love and passion between human beings and the gods. She became additionally associated with fertility and preference.

Mythology and Legends of Aphrodite

Aphrodite changed into concerned in numerous mythological stories, which incorporates the story of Pygmalion, who fell in love with a statue he carved and which Aphrodite converted proper into a actual girl. Another incredible tale is that of Eros and Psyche, which explored the subject count of love and take into account.

Worship and Cult

Aphrodite have become worshiped during Ancient Greece, and loads of temples have been committed to her. The town of Cnidos had a famous statue of Aphrodite, sculpted thru Praxiteles , which have become considered one of the maximum beautiful representations of the goddess.

Ares - The God of War

In this financial ruin, we are capable of find out the area of Ares, the god of struggle, violence, and carnage in Greek mythology. Get ready to satisfy the deity who personifies the brutality of armed war.

The Origin of Ares

Ares changed into the son of Zeus and Hera, making him one of the fundamental gods of Olympus. However, he have become often taken into consideration unpopular amongst gods and mortals alike due to his violent nature and choice for battle.

The God of War and Violence

Ares become the god of conflict in his most brutal shape. Unlike Athena, who represented approach and statistics in warfare, Ares personified violence, chaos and bloodlust on the battlefield.

Relationship with Aphrodite

One of the maximum famous testimonies concerning Ares is his love affair with Aphrodite, the goddess of affection and beauty, who end up married to Hephaestus, the god of blacksmiths. His novel illustrates the connection among love and warfare, highlighting the duality of human nature.

Participation in Mythological Battles

Ares became worried in plenty of mythological battles, preventing alongside the Trojans in the Trojan War and assisting wonderful heroes and gods in violent conflicts.

The Adoration of Ares

Ares come to be now not as extensively worshiped in Ancient Greece as compared to exclusive gods, as his bloodthirsty nature come to be no longer seemed sympathetically with the aid of using the Greeks. However, a few town-states , which includes Sparta, revered Ares as a navy protector.

Mythology and Legends of Ares

Ares has regarded in numerous mythological testimonies, often as the antagonist. His bloodlust and impulsiveness regularly delivered him into struggle with unique gods and heroes.

Hermes - The Divine Messenger

In this monetary smash, we're capable of discover the exciting international of Hermes, the god of communication, mischief, and vacationers in Greek mythology. Get organized to meet the divine messenger and the god of trickery.

The Origin of Hermes

Hermes changed into the son of Zeus and the nymph Maia. From the start, he confirmed a curious and agile nature, dispositions that would define him in the end of his existence.

The Divine Messenger

Hermes become the messenger of the gods, answerable for transmitting messages and messages amongst Olympus and the mortal global. He changed into additionally the god of tourists, traders and thieves.

The Caduceus and the Wings on the Feet

Hermes became regularly depicted with a caduceus, a employees entwined with serpents, which symbolized negotiation and international own family participants. Furthermore, he had wings on his ft that allowed him to move notably brief, making him an green messenger.

www.ingramcontent.com/pod-product-compliance
Lightning Source LLC
Chambersburg PA
CBHW071334120626
46546CB00002B/556